WOMAN
WHY ARE YOU WEEPING?

A discussion
on Women's Ordination
in the Roman Catholic Church
in the context
of
WOW 2001 DUBLIN

WOMAN
WHY ARE YOU WEEPING?

A discussion
on Women's Ordination
in the Roman Catholic Church
in the context
of
WOW 2001 DUBLIN

WOMAN
WHY ARE YOU WEEPING?

A discussion on Women's Ordination
in the Roman Catholic Church
in the context of
WOW 2001 DUBLIN

Foreword by Dr. John Wijngaards

Dr. James Kottoor

Media House
Delhi
2002

2002

Woman why are you weeping?

A discussion on Women's Ordination in the Roman Catholic Church in the context of WOW 2001 Dublin

Dr. James Kottoor

Copyright: Dr. James Kottoor (2002)
E-mail: jkottoor@vsnl.com

Published by: MEDIA HOUSE
375-A, Pocket 2, Mayur Vihar Phase-I, Delhi - 110 091
Phone: 011-2750667, Telefax: 011-2751317
E-mail: mediabooks@hotmail.com

ISBN: 81-7495-111-3

Printed at: MEDIA HOUSE
A-1/3 Surya Nagar, Ghaziabad, U.P. 201 011, INDIA,
Ph: 0120-4629921, Fax: 0120-4629008,
E-mail: mediahouse@vsnl.com

Contents

Dedication To **The Word Made Flesh** — James Kottoor 8

Introduction — James Kottoor 9

Foreword — Dr. John Wijngaards 15

Part I: Presentation of the State of the Question
(From a Theological, Scriptural, Magisterial and Traditional points of view)

1. Women Priests in Catholic Church *(Exposition of the State of the Question: Public Opinion in Church, Mary's Priestly Role, Women in N. Testament, Women admitted to Deaconate, Assessment of Theologians)* — James Kottoor 22

2. Cross Currents: *a) Vatican's View; b) Theological Musings; c) A President's View; d) Anatomy of the Conference* — James Kottoor 35

3. Interview with 4 Speakers:*(Dr. Wijngaards, Sr. Joan Chittister, Mairead Maguire & Rev.Rose Hudson)* — James Kottoor 40

4. Women Theologians Seek to end Male Monopoly; Women Priests in Early Church; Women Priests Today — ICAN Reports 46

5. ·Some say 'Yes' others say 'no': Bishops, Rector, Professor, Sisters, Laity — Suresh Pallivathukkal 50

6. 14 Indian Sisters' Letter to Pope in 1994 on *Ordinatio Sacerdotalis* 54

Part II: What took place during the 3-day Conference
(Speeches, discussions, resolutions and outside reactions)

7.   A Celebration of Women's Call to a Renewed Priesthood in the Catholic Church, *Inaugural Address*
                                    — Mairead Corrigan Maguire 61

8.   Woman Beautifully made in God's Image, *Keynote Address*
                                    — Rev. Rose Hudson Wilkin 67

9.   Ecumenical Perspective: Church Unity or WOW more Important? *(Summary report on Aruna Gnanadason's Paper)*
                                    — James Kottoor 72

10. Preaching Equality, Practicing Inequality *(Report of Sr. Joan's Speech, from Dublin)*   — James Kottoor 77

11. Nuns Defy Vatican Ban *(Report on Vatican Censure and Irish reaction)*   — James Kottoor 86

12. Discerning the Spirit's New Creation, *Speech*
                                    — Dr. John Wijngaards 89

13. International Panel Presentation: *(Presentation by delegates from: S. Africa, Uganda, Japan, Hungary, Brazil and letter of support from Germany)*   114

14. WOW Passes 11 Resolutions *(Report from Dublin)*
                                    — James Kottoor 125

Part III: Aftermath of the Conference
(Vatican and Indian reaction and Evaluation of the Conference)

15. No Punitive Action from Vatican *(Article in IC reporting and commenting on the Press Release (full text) of Prioress Christine Vladimiroff of Sr. Joan)*   — James Kottoor   129

16. Evaluation of WOW *(Soline Vatinel, the spokesperson for*

*the Conference makes a personal evaluation one month
after the conference)*   — Soline Vatinel   133

17.   Woman, Why are you weeping? Discovering Christ in the tomb
      of Church *(Round up of the Conference)*
                                           — James Kottoor   138

18.   Opinion Poll Results   — Suresh Pallivathukkal   144

19.   Letters to Editor in IC *(Readers' Reaction for and against
      to reports on Dublin Conference)*   150

20.   Critics Help Fortify Weak Defenses; Critical Loyalty and Loyal
      Criticism, not blind 'Yes'   — James Kottoor   170

21.   Tea-shop Chats *(Religious Satire: Imaginary conversation
      indulged in by imaginary persons in a Tea shop in India
      on Women Priests)*   — Anoop Dev   176

22.   Epilogue   — James Kottoor   183

Part IV: Appendix
(Full text of Conference Papers of Sr. Joan and Ms Aruna Gnanadason)

23.   Discipleship for a Priestly People in a Priestless World
                                          — Sr. Joan Chittister   189

24.   We will Pour our Ointment on the Feet of the Church.
                                       — Aruna Gnanadason   204

Humbly

Dedicated

To

The Word

That was in the beginning

The Word

That was with God

The Word

That became Flesh

To

Abide with every man, woman and child

Who welcomes this Word

For the Purpose

of being shared with the rest of humanity

as

The Word of Power with the Power of the Word!

Introduction

What would be the thinking of people on women's ordination in the Roman Catholic Church twenty years from now? That question has relevance only if we place before ourselves what the current thinking on the subject is at various levels in the Church, in various regions around the world. This is precisely what the Dublin Conference on Women's Ordination Worldwide (WOW), the first of its kind held from June 28 to July 1st, 2001 has done. This book is all about that: what preceded the conference, what took place during the conference and what followed the conference.

Looking at the subject from a global perspective Women's Ordination (WO) has been both a topic of heated debate and a topic of no consequence depending on the inroads the subject has make into the minds of Roman Catholics around the globe. Thus it may be safe to say that it has today become a burning issue for a vast number of Catholics in the west led by concerned, convinced and articulate sections in many countries in Europe and the Americas while it still remains an issue of little importance in the East, especially in many Asian countries like India, except for a minority of theologically better informed Christians in these countries. In other words the Dublin conference was a gathering spearheaded by the theologically conscientised Christians from all over the world, to give visibility to the importance and seriousness of the topic and to build up a healthy public opinion in the church by getting involved all sections of Christians from all over the world, especially the less informed.

If we narrow it down to a purely Indian perspective, how relevant was this conference and how meaningful is this subject to Christians in general and Roman Catholics in particular in India? To a vast majority it must have come like a bolt from the blue, a shock treatment waking them up for the first time to the manifold, undreamt-of implications of a priestly ministry for the women folk who, all admit are more spiritually oriented than men and who comprise half of humanity. Take for example the prospects it opens up for the nearly 80,000 religious sisters in India, whose selfless spiritual mission of mercy is the most appreciated across all community barriers but who are at times described in some quarters as the bonded labourers of the Catholic Church because of the stepmotherly treatment meted out to them from their male dominated counter parts. The public discussion has at least given a new fillip to the realistic and realizable expectations of many of these concerned women and men in the country. In this sense it was a wake-up call to a priestly ministry and mission addressed to a priestly and spiritually oriented people coming from a priest-less west steeped in materialistic and consumerist pursuits.

First Part

With a view to leading the general public from the known to the unknown, from the easily understandable to the hardly digestible, the book is divided into three main parts. The first part comprising chapters from 1 to 6 exposes the state of the question from the points of view of the advocates of WO and its opponents at various levels – scriptural, theological, magisterial, institutional and traditional. The first chapter gives a brief exposition of the state of the question from these various scholarly angles. The second chapter brings into focus certain clash of views at the theological and magisterial levels in the Church. The Third chapter, an interview with experts in the field, explains the relevance of this subject to the Indian public in preparation for the unfolding conference. The fourth chapter exposes the thinking and approach to WO in the early church and at present. The fifth chapter is a letter of Oct.31st, 1994, addressed to the present Holy Father by a group of 14 Indian Sisters just five months after the publication of the Apostolic letter *Ordinatio Sacerotalis* of May 1994, excluding women from ordained ministry in the Roman Catholic church. It is proof that a theologically alert section of women in the church in India, known as WORTH (=Women Religious Theologizing) was already ceased of the seriousness of the subject and was even ahead of many of their counter parts in other countries in reacting respectfully and forcefully to the Papal teaching citing scriptural and theological reasons.

Second Part

The second part of the book from chapters 7 to 14 is all about the light and sound displayed by an ecumenical leading lights — speakers, experts and international spokespersons at the conference hall in Dublin and some of the repercussions it produced in the secular press as reported by this writer, who happened to be one of the three invitees from India. While the inaugural address(Chapter 7) was given by a Roman Catholic Peace Prize Laureate, Mairead Corrigan Maguire, the slot of the Keynote address(8 & 9) was amply filled by contributions from Rev. Rose Hudson Wilkin, an Anglican of Jamaican origin and Ms.Aruna Gnanadason of the Church of South India, who circulated her paper for the benefit of the participants since she had to bow out of the conference due to various pressures brought upon her. Chapter 10 highlights the substance of the star speaker at the conference, the Benedictine Sister Joan Chittister, whose attendance created suspense and controversy because of the instructions from the Vatican to her through her Prioress not to attend the conference. This provided juicy news for the Irish dailies to come up with Headlines like: Nuns Defy Vatican Ban (Chapter 11). Chapter 12 gives the full text of the Scholarly speech by Dr. John Wijngaards, who is an expert and an articulate advocate of WO. His elaborate and well documented website on WO has provided most of the background data for this book. The international panel discussion (Chapter 13) gives the reader a taste of the rumblings on WO in some of the countries in Africa, Asia and Europe. The 11 resolutions passed by the conference bring down the curtain on the Dublin show.

Third Part

The third part of the book titled the aftermath of the conference from chapters 15 to 22 sum up the outcome of the conference. The full text of the letter of Prioress Vladimiroff (Chapter 14) provides food for thought or literally fodder for chewing the cud for those who want to delve deep into the true concept of obedience and authority that attempts at mind control. The wise decision of the Vatican not to take any punitive action may be seen as a victory for sanity and sobriety and an implicit positive response to the first resolution of the conference. Chapters 15 and 16 form parts of a piece, evaluation of WOW. Ms.Soline Vatinel the spokesperson of the Conference makes a personal evaluation one month after the conference. The following chapter: *Woman: Why are you weeping?* makes an assessment of the central issues addressed by the conference and the net gains flowing out from that exercise.

Since the image of the weeping woman at the tomb has come to represent the sorry plight of half of humanity today in the Roman Catholic Church gathered in Dublin to celebrate, it was chosen as the title of this book, as also suggested by the Editor in Chief of Indian Currents (IC) Dr. Xavier Vadakkekara. But the net gain of the conference was the victory for the freedom of conscience, freedom of expression and freedom of debate without sacrificing either loyalty or criticism. Since the theological and scriptural foundation of this universal human right is to be located in the unfathomable, soul searching, breathtaking and earthshaking explosion of the mystery of the Word made Flesh, this book is prayerfully dedicated to that Word Incarnate that continues to get reincarnated every time an honest truth is conceived in any human mind and freely expressed without fear or favour for the benefit of MAN, that is, for the liberation of the WHOLE man and ALL men by truth conceived, expressed and shared freely. The explosion of the incarnational mystery was like the dropping of a heavenly bombshell on to this earth, not for its destruction or desecration but for its recreation and rejuvenisation of the entire universe. Every honest truth conceived is to be expressed and shared for the benefit of all humanity.

The following three chapters, Opinion Poll by Suresh Pallivathukal, letters to the Editor from a wide variety of Indian reading public expressing their honest appreciation of all well as pointed criticisms, give an indication of the emerging (*Sensus Fidelium*) honest thinking of the Church in India. Most important in this section are the letters to the editor of IC – one solitary honest bishop setting the edifying example of speaking up his considered views and ever so many from among the laity speaking up their minds. What we have from the vast number of priests, sisters and religious is their intriguingly eloquent silence, except for a solitary priest stationed in Rome.

A chapter on the Teashop chats is included just to remind all that we should learn to laugh at ourselves even in the midst of high and heavenly discussion, that we should not take our views and even our considered convictions too seriously as if we are all indispensable and infallible humans. An epilogue is added as the 22nd chapter to give an indication of the direction of the possible thinking on this and related issues twenty or forty years from now. The appendix carries the full texts(Chapters 23 & 24) of the Star speaker of the Conference and Aruna Gnanadason, attached to the WCC, providential for the benefit of those who want to make an in depth study.

Providential

Finally a word about this book itself. I preplanned neither this book nor my trip to Dublin. To be honest I was a very reluctant rebel kicking against the goad and finally giving in to well-meaning pressures brought upon me. The only things I don't believe in are accidents. Everything has a definite purpose in God's providential plan. So I see the publication of this book in this light. I take this opportunity to thank Sr.Myra Poole the Organiser and the stalwarts of BASIC (Brothers and Sisters in Christ) Mr. Colm Holmes and Soline Vatinel, who invited me to the Conference although I knew none of them before. But I am specially indebted to my long time friend Dr. Wijngaards who made my work of covering the conference easy through his timely suggestion to study his website on Women's Ordination. I also thank him for writing a foreword to this book.

But the credit for the very idea of bringing out a book of this type, its cover design, layout and final production must go to the Editor of the IC and Media House, at whose suggestion I took up this work. At the end of it all, I feel relieved that I have got out of my chest a big or small, a good or bad egg. How nourishing is the omelet prepared out of this egg, it for the readers to taste and see. But it is hoped that it will not be easy to read it and forget it because of the freedom of conscience and expression this book preaches and practices from start to finish as part of the inalienable heritage of the freedom of the children of God in the Roman Catholic Church. It is therefore the fervent and humble prayer of this scribe that this book may help every honest WORD conceived to become flesh for the benefit of all!

Santhi Bavan   Dr. James Kottoor,
42/1435 Thammanam   January 15, 2002
Ernakulam, Kochi - 682 032
Ph: 0484 - 344679
E-mail: jkottoor@vsnl.com

Foreword

Beware! You are opening a dangerous book. If you are willing to think critically, this book may shake your faith - - but only to rid your mind of traditional litter and root your faith more firmly into your deepest Christian convictions. For, believe it or not, women as much as men are called to be priests: to preside at the Eucharist, to hear confessions, to anoint the sick.

This book documents the proceedings of an International Catholic Congress that directly challenged the Congregation for Doctrine in Rome. In recent years the Vatican has repeatedly declared that women will never be ordained priests. It cannot be done, it stated: "Christ has ruled it out. Tradition always forbade it. The Church does not have the power to change this. Women *cannot* be priests. That's it! The discussion is over. Catholics will never, never, never see a woman priest at the altar!"

The Dublin Conference with 350 Catholic representatives from 26 countries said just the opposite. Women *will* be ordained in the Catholic Church. "This is according to Christ's will. Reluctance to ordain women in the past was due to social and theological prejudice. In this matter, as in many others, the Catholic Church needs to be reformed."

Then whom to believe? Why should we pay attention to dissenting voices when the weight of Catholic tradition and Catholic authority seem ranged against? But judging 'weight' can be deceptive.

A small tremor can herald the unleashing of a huge earthquake. A puff of smoke from the top of a sleeping volcano may announce the explosion of a pent-up sea of red hot lava. What are the facts?

The source of infallibility

It's all a question of awareness. In Catholic communities where people still learn the catechism by heart and do as they are told, the monopoly men hold on administering the sacraments is still taken for granted. But in all countries where people have had access to higher education and have had an opportunity to study the past critically, two-thirds of Catholics have become convinced that the ban against women priests has no legitimate foundation. And since education and critical judgement are increasing everywhere, the tide of this new awareness is becoming unstoppable.

A Catholic who studies the history of the ban on women priests will discover glaring anomalies. If, moreover, that same person in prayer probes the depth of one's consciousness, he/she suddenly finds right there, in the heart of our Catholic belief, that it is *obvious* that women should be ordained. Anything less would contradict the fact that God created both men and women in God's image, that God loves both without preference, that Christ made both men and women full and equal members of his kingdom, that a woman can be deputed to represent Christ as a man can. All the theological reasonings of the past are suddenly understood to be no more than lame excuses, a cover up for the secular male domination that infected our Catholic community in previous centuries.

The point is that ordinary Catholics do not need professional theological training to grasp what is at stake. Once made aware, they know what their Catholic faith in their hearts tells them. In theological language this is known as the 'sense of the faithful', 'the Catholic sense' or 'the gospel of the heart'. The new awareness that we see erupting among Catholics all over the world is a manifestation of this sense of faith.

And here the story becomes really interesting. For Catholics often think that infallibility moves from the top down: from the Pope to the bishops, then descending down to the faithful. But the Second Vatican Council teaches the reverse. The true carrier of the Church's infallible doctrine is the sense of faith in the heart of believers. The Pope and the assembled bishops have a privileged role in discerning and declaring what is part of that infallible doctrine, but they cannot make it up, nor do they receive it from on high. With prayer, humility and careful study they have to discover, every time again, what lies hidden as a treasure, always old and always new, in the heart of the Christian faithful.

At the international conference in Dublin, ordinary Catholics spoke from the depth of their Christian commitment: theologians, lay people, religious, spiritual authors, journalists, parish assistants and teachers. They manifested what lives in Catholic communities all over the world, expressing more articulately what others feel instinctively, proclaiming that the exclusion of women from the priesthood conflicts with the core of their Catholic identity. And this is where discussion begins.

The ding-dong of debate

The phase of argumentation can be exasperating. Imagine Nirmala fending off objections put forward by her traditionalist friend Thomas.

Thomas: "The Church has never ordained women."

Nirmala: "No? Then what about women deacons in the early Church?"

Thomas: "That was just a minor order ....

Nirmala: "It was not, for nine centuries women were ordained deacon through exactly the same rite as male deacons were. So women were ordained!"

Thomas: "But that was only the diaconate. Not the priesthood."

Nirmala: "Ok, it was not the priesthood. But remember, the diaconate belongs to the sacrament of holy orders, as the Council of Trent defined. Women therefore *did* receive the sacrament of ordination - - and if they could be deacons, they can be priests!"

Thomas: "At the Eucharist a priest represents Christ. But women are only women and Christ was a man. How can a woman priest represent Christ . . . ?"

I will not continue this sample argumentation here, though studying the arguments is a necessary evil at some stage of one's journey of discovery. What is important to note is that the vast majority of Catholic theologians have come to the conclusion that the official reasons for which women have been excluded from ordination are simply invalid. The ban against women priests is a cuckoo's egg laid into the nest of Catholic tradition by a pagan parent bird; the law of ancient Rome that denied any public responsibility to women.

Once the arguments have been dismantled, a new phase begins. One begins to be worried, *concerned*. What about the further implications?

● If women can be validly and legitimately ordained priests, does integrity not demand that we honestly concede it?

● Does the Catholic Church, and in particular its teaching authority, not lose all its credibility by maintaining a position that is manifestly untrue?

● And what about the damage done to the community of the faithful by withholding from it the valuable priestly ministry that could be given to it by women?

● Is it not a sin to continue stifling the Holy Spirit who calls so many women to her priestly service?

If women can be ordained priests, it is a matter of life or death for the health of the Church that the ancient prejudices be dropped and women be admitted to all ranks of holy orders. This overriding concern puts the Dublin conference within the right context.

Hope for the future?

I highly commend Indian Currents and Media House for bringing this vital question to the attention of Catholics in India. Whether one agrees to the ordination of women or not, no thinking Catholic should remain unaware of what the discussion is all about. And acquaintance with the facts of the case will, no doubt, make many people sit up and take note. Old prejudices live on as long as ignorance is allowed to last.

As never before the Church is in need of prophets who dare to speak out in spite of established wisdom and in defiance of the 'party line' imposed from above. "Do not try to suppress the Spirit or treat the gift of prophecy with contempt!", Paul urged the turbulent community at Thessalonika (1 Thess 5,19). He certainly would back up prophecy that challenges authority. For writing to the Corinthians, he attributed to prophets a task different from that of teachers and apostles (1 Cor 12,27-30). And did Paul himself, in front of the whole Christian community of Antioch, not unambiguously oppose the leader of the apostles "for Peter was manifestly in the wrong" (Gal 2,11)?

But what about the prophets of our Christian community today? Will the leaders of the Church give heed to the voices of prophecy contained in this book?

> I look at the face of older women
> wrinkled but dignified
> silently suffering the disgrace
> of centuries of prejudice.

> I look at the face of younger women
> radiant with a vision
> that one day they will minister
> Christ's priestly love
> to those in need of spiritual care.

I look at the face of Church leaders
as I desperately search for
signs of hope
- - all I see is the stern frown of men
who punish and condemn.

And yet, I live in hope.
I wish I had more reason to hope.
I fear I have lost
the ability to hope with confidence.

Church leaders who punish and condemn
Lord, crack the shell of institutional bias
so that our hopes and visions
may become a reality,
so that the groaning of your Spirit
in the hearts of your people
may bear fruit.

John Wijngaards

Part I

Presentation
of the State
of the Question

1

Women's Ordination Worldwide 2001

Dublin meet on Women Priests in Catholic Church!

Dr.James Kottoor

"Now is the time: A celebration of women's call to a renewed priesthood in the Catholic Church," was the theme of the first-ever international conference on the subject convened by Women's Ordination Worldwide (WOW) in Dublin, Ireland, from June 29th to July 1st. Mairead Corrigan Maguire, Nobel Peace Prize Laureate, author of Vision of Peace and co-founder of the Peace People inaugurated the conference.

WOW was founded in 1996 as a collaboration of women's ordination groups/ movements/organizations all around the world with Sr. Myra Poole of the Catholic Women's Ordination in Great Britain as the chairperson (e-mail: myra.poole@virgin.net). Groups in different countries work for the inclusion of women in the renewed priestly ministry in the Catholic Church. The conference was hosted by BASIC (Brothers and sisters in Christ) the Catholic organization in Ireland the host country. An inscription on the letterhead of BASIC: "*Praying and working for the ordination of women in the Roman Catholic church,*" highlighted the spirit which animated the organizers.

Prominent speakers included Rev. Rose Hudson-Wilkin, an Evangelist ordained priest in 1994 and serving Lichfield Diocese,

England as Vicar of Holy Trinity, Dalston and All Saints, Haggerston in the London Diocese. She is the Chairperson for the National Committee for minority ethnic Anglican concerns and a member of the Broadcasting Standards Commission and represented the WCC meeting in Harare in 1998.

Sr.Joan Chittister of Pennsylvania, USA who spoke on Ordained Ministry for a Priestly People, is a social psychologist, international lecturer and author of over twenty books, the recent ones being: *The Story of Ruth; Twelve Moments in Every Woman's Life; Illuminated Life; In search of Belief; Heart of Flesh; A Feminist Spirituality for women and Men.* A member of the Benedictine Sisters of Erie, she is the executive director of Benetvision: A Resource and Research Centre for Contemporary Spirituality. She is a past president of the Conference of American Benedictine Prioresses and the Leadership Conference of Women Religious and has taught at all educational levels.

Dr.John Wijngaards, who exposed his personal story and explained why he has been engaged in this movement, is a graduate from the Biblical Institute with a doctorate from the Gregorian University, Rome. A missionary in India for 14 years, he was Vicar General of the Mill Hill Missionaries from 1976-82, and was director of Housetop in London, which designed courses for adult faith formation, used in all continents. After becoming an outspoken campaigner for women priests in the Catholic Church, he resigned from his priestly ministry in 1998. As a scholar he painstakingly dismantles the traditional objections to women priests through his renowned web site: www.womenpriests.org

Public Opinion in Church

The Dublin conference was a public demonstration of the growing groundswell of public opinion in the Church on Women's Ordination to Priesthood.

In the spirit of Vatican Council document *Gaudium et Spes, no 6:* "All the faithful, both clerical and lay, should be accorded a lawful freedom of inquiry and of thought, and the freedom to express their minds humbly and courageously about those matters in which they enjoy competence," and *Inter Mirifica No.8,* on the crucial role to be played by *public opinion* in today's society: "Public opinion exercises enormous influence nowadays over the lives, private or public, of all citizens, no matter what their walk in life. It is therefore necessary that all members of society meet the demands of justice and charity in this domain. They should help, through the means of social communication, in the formation and diffusion of sound public opinion," both theologians and lay people in the Catholic church have been discussing for long the possibility and necessity of opening the doors of priestly ministry also to women.

These discussions trace their source of inspiration to the pre-eminent role played by Mary, the mother of Christ in the redemptive work which culminated in Christ's crucifixion on Calvary; the priestly titles and honours attributed to her by the saints and Fathers of the church in the early centuries; the place and role accorded to women by Christ and the Apostles in their time; the practice of conferring Diaconate to women in the Early church, and many arguments of contemporary theologians.

All Christians share in Jesus' priesthood through the so-called common priesthood of the faithful. Tradition however asserted much more about Mary and this can be seen especially in the way in which Mary is seen and portrayed as a sacrificial priest, on a par with and parallel to Eucharistic ministers. Mary has been called explicitly a "sacrificing priest", and a "sacrificer". Here below are just a few samples culled from the wide variety of information available for all to see on the website.

Mary's Priestly Role

"Mary could not escape from Calvary because God had given her the mission to remain there as priest, victim and mediatrix. She had to stay on Calvary, next to the cross and in the heart of her

Son. She stood up straight on Calvary and undertook her function as priest. She stood next to the cross and fulfilled the role of a victim. She stayed in the heart of Jesus and acquitted herself of the task of mediatrix: strong in her first task, faithful to her second, devoted in her third . . . Mary had to fulfill her first task, that of being a priest." St. Antonio Maria Claret (1807-1870).

"Three elements belong to the priesthood and episcopacy: the call, the role of intercession, and sacrifice (Hebr 5, 1) . . . [With regard to intercession] as Son of God Christ has all power over God. Our Lady too, because she is the true Mother of God, has all power over God. And if the prayers and intercessions of Christ are heard on account of the fact that he is the Son, those of Our Lady will not be less heard, and are even heard with more surety because of the fact that she is his Mother. Therefore it is crystal clear that in Mary we find overwhelmingly the second quality required for the dignity of a bishop!" Antonio Vieira (1608 - 1697).

"In the incarnation Mary was as it were the altar on which the victim was laid down and on which he was kindled through the flame of her love; at the presentation, she has become as the priest who in fact offered her son; and at the redemption as *the sacrificial priest* who immolated him." Auguste Nicolas (1858)

"Just as she has been the first priest to bring forth Jesus Christ, she will be the first priest to offer him. She was the first sacrificer as she had been the first consecrator . . . On top of the holy mount of Calvary, she stays upright in the posture of a sacrificer standing before the altar, that is: the cross, where the first Mass is celebrated and where redemption was accomplished . . . Mary is the priestess *[sacerdotissa]* of justice because she did not spare her own Son, but stood by the Cross, not, as blessed Ambrose says, to just see the death of her Son, not to witness the suffering of her Son, but to look forward to the salvation of the human race, prepared herself to offer the Son of God for the salvation of the world". St. Antoninus of Florence (1389-1459)

She also experienced the martyrdom of her own will. "Because she stood next to the cross out of her own free will, as Ambrose says; ready for the salvation of the human race, to also undergo suffering herself, if it had pleased the divine will: offering, as a high priest, the beloved and unique child of her heart, more perfect than Abraham offered Isaac; [she offered her son] for the salvation of people, and interceding for them." Jan Mombaer (1501)

"If it had been necessary . . .Mary would herself have offered the nails, handed the hammer, readied the cords to tie her Son to the sacrificial wood, as Abraham had done. She has sacrificed him for us." Joachim Ventura (1792-1861)

Mary brought Christ down to earth by her word, as priests do at consecration. She made the Word through her word – fiat. "Mary is also something greater than temples or tabernacles, . . . she is priest. What do we mean with a priest of the new covenant? A priest has the power to mystically produce the body of the Lord giving that body its sacramental form . . . I allow myself to say that Mary is the first to say Mass, by agreeing to the Incarnation and so preparing the victim . . . Mary fulfils in advance the sacrifice of the cross by preparing what is required for it . . . . More than any priest she can point at her crucified Son and say: 'This is my body!' Mary is therefore not a priest who does not share in the sacrifice, but a priest who puts herself into the victim who is the heavenly bread." Bishop Nazlian (1914)

"This [to have an image of Mary suspended behind the altar] is a profitable arrangement so that the priest, while celebrating the sacred mysteries, can look at Mary and measure the quality of this woman to whom it was entrusted to make the Word, through her own word. The priest should reflect on what the priest should be like who on his word, or rather on the word of Christ spoken through him, makes from the substance of bread and wine the body and blood of Christ." St. Antoninus of Florence. (1389 – 1459)

Her priestly ordination took place when Jesus was conceived. "No other predisposition necessary for the priesthood appears more clearly in the Virgin than being called by God.... That great calling made her the Mother of God, just as a priest's calling makes him, to some extent, the source and the father of the same Son of God since it gives the priest the power to produce Christ's body through words, as the Virgin has done." Saint-Cyran.

These and ever so many quotations from Church's spokespersons are exposed on the web site to fashion and strengthen a public opinion in the church 1) that if priests in the church today transform bread and wine into the body and blood of Christ during the Holy Sacrifice of the Mass, Mary was the first Priestess who did it in an eminent way through her *Fiat* which caused the Word to become flesh in her womb at the Annunciation; 2) that she alone more than anyone else could say pointing to Christ: He is truly flesh of my flesh and blood of my blood; 3) that she by doing the heart-rending act of trudging the way of the cross and embracing the blood drenched foot of the cross on Calvary became both queen of priests and Priestess par excellence in a way far superior to Abraham who did not have to sacrifice his son Isaac; 4) that if her being a woman did not prevent her from doing all that, it should not prevent today's women fired with zeal to follow in the footsteps of the Lord, from doing even priestly ministry like Mary.

The statement of St. Paul, Gal.3.27: "All baptized in Christ, you have all clothed yourselves in Christ, and there are no more distinctions between Jew and Greek, slave and free, *male and female*, but all of you are one in Christ Jesus," is cited to fight all forms of discrimination based on *sex* and Peter 2.9: "But you are a chosen race, a *royal priesthood,* a consecrated nation, a people set apart to sing the praises of God who called you out of the darkness into his wonderful light," is quoted to highlight the call to the priesthood extended to all the baptized both men and women.

Women in New Testament

Foot-washing ministry was central to the preaching and practice of Christ. It was a member of the womenfolk that excelled in
it. This is what the story of Mary of Magdala at the house of Simon
(Lk.7.36) demonstrates. Women were very closely associated with
Jesus on his apostolic journeys. This should imply the possibility of
a similar participation of women in the era of the Church. While all
four Gospels affirm that women played a special part in Jesus' life,
it is particularly notable in Luke's Gospel, which records episodes
not found in the other Gospel accounts. He introduces Elizabeth
(Lk. 1, 5-45), the prophetess Anna (Lk 2, 36-38), the widow of
Naim (Lk 7, 11-17), the women who ministered unto Jesus (Lk 8,
1-3), the woman who was bent over (Lk 13, 38-42) and the weeping women of Jerusalem (Lk 23, 27-31). Luke preserved two
special parables involving women: the housewife who lost a
drachma (Lk 15, 8-10) and the tenacious widow (Lk 18, 1-8).
Women also mentioned in the other Gospels, receive special focus with Luke: Mary Magdalene (Lk 7, 36-50), Mary and Martha
(Lk 10, 38-42) and the poor widow who offered two coins in the
temple (Lk 21, 1-4). Jesus' relationship to women is an outspoken theme of Luke's Gospel.

Why did Luke focus attention on the role played by women in
Jesus' life? Obviously here, as in the other cases, Luke acted in
response to a need in the early Church. In many communities
women played a leading role. Apollos' conversion at Ephesus was
as much due to Priscilla as to Aquila (Acts 18, 18-26). In Corinth
it was Chloë who sent messengers to Paul to inform him about
problems in the Church (1 Cor 1, 11). The community of Cenchreae
had a lady deacon, 'Phoebe our fellow-christian' (Rom 16, 1-2). At
Philippi, where Luke worked a long time in the apostolate, we find
mention of three prominent ladies: Lydia, who ran a prosperous business in purple dresses and in whose house the local community met
(Acts 16, 14-15); Euodia and Syntyche about whom Paul could

say 'these women who shared my struggles in the cause of the Gospel' (Phil 4, 2-3). It is obvious that these women and others whose names have not been recorded, were concerned about their own specific role in the Christian community.

When recalling incidents of Jesus' life involving women, Luke has a very rich message to give. According to research scholars women are equal recipients of Jesus' grace. Like men, women too should be converted (Mary Magdalene), listen to Jesus' word (Mary and Martha), pray with perseverance (the tenacious widow), and share in his sufferings and cross (Lk 23, 49). The role of being a mother, with its sorrows and joys, is reflected on in persons such as the widow of Naim, Elizabeth and Our Lady. Jesus takes examples from women's everyday tasks: drawing water from the well, grinding corn with the millstones, sweeping the house, mixing leaven through the dough, and preparing food for guests. Jesus had observed such activities and invested some of them with profound symbolic meaning. In these and many other ways Luke's passages on women yield an unexpectedly rich treasury of pointers and reflections.

These pointers according to the author of the article in the web site should lead the way for the emergence of women priests in the Church. The fact that Christ chose only men to function on his apostolic team, according to him, was not determined by his own specific preference, but by the social pressure of his time. In the circumstances Christ could not have appointed women to a priestly task. But in no way did he at any time rule out the possibility of women being ordained priests.

Women admitted to Diaconate

It is also pointed out that there are ever so many women who were ordained as deacons in the early Church on the same basis as men. For the sacrament of holy orders has three levels: episcopacy, priesthood and diaconate. Anyone who receives any of the three is consecrated to the ministerial priesthood, as the Council of Trent defined it. "But were women ordained as real deacons - into a sacramental diaconate 'tied theologically to the Holy Spirit', to borrow Cardinal Castrillon Hoyos's words?" asks Dr.Wijngaards writing on women deacons (*The Tablet, May 8, 1999)* and says:

"The answer lies in precious Greek and Syriac manuscripts concealed in dusty libraries, but now to be made accessible to all via the Internet *(www.womenpriests.org)*. They contain ancient ordination rituals for male and female deacons, documenting the Church's practice from the fourth to the eighth centuries AD, and confirming the oldest ordination prayers already found in the *Apostolic Constitutions,* a so-called fourth-century "church order" with regulations for discipline and liturgy.... if the Church ordained women deacons and male deacons with exactly the same sacramental signs, how could anyone say that one - the diaconate of men - is sacramental, and the other - that of women - is not? Do not the severe words of the Council of Trent apply here? 'If anyone says that, through sacred ordination, the Holy Spirit is not given, and that therefore the bishop says in vain: 'Receive the Holy Spirit' . . . Let him be anathema." (constitution on Holy Orders, canon 4)

He gives also an abridged version of the ordination prayer for a woman deacon: "Holy and omnipotent Lord, through the birth of your only Son from a virgin according to his human nature, you have sanctified the female sex. You grant not only to men, but also to women, the grace and outpouring of the Holy Spirit. Please, Lord, look on this your maidservant and dedicate her to the task of your diaconate, and pour out into her the rich and abundant giving of your Holy Spirit."

According to Dr. Wijngaards, "In the West, the 'woman's deaconate' continued to exist until the early Middle Ages as a 'blessing' imparted to abbesses. It was but a feeble shadow of the real thing that had existed in the East..... St Chrysostom at Constantinople had 40 women deacons attached to the basilica of Hagia Sophia, as well as 100 male deacons. From the correspondence of the Fathers we know a good many by name: Salvina, to whom St Jerome wrote; Macrina, the sister of St Basil the Great; Anastasia, an assistant of Severus Bishop of Antioch...So here we have proof that women were admitted to holy orders for centuries, under the sanction of ecumenical councils, producing ordained ministers who confirmed in their own person the equality of men and women in Christ."

Assessment of Theologians

All this is being done in spite of the Papal Encyclical '*Ordinatio Sacerdotalis*' of May 22nd.1994: "She (the curch) holds that it is not admissible to ordain women to the priesthood, for very fundamental reasons. These reasons include: the example recorded in the Sacred Scriptures of Christ choosing his Apostles only from among men; the constant practice of the Church, which has imitated Christ in choosing only men; and her living teaching authority which has consistently held that the exclusion of women from the priesthood is in accordance with God's plan for his Church," and the statement of the Congregation for the Doctrine of Faith of Nov.18, 1995 declaring that the exclusion of women from priestly ordination has been infallibly decided by the 'ordinary universal magisterium' of the Church. How do theologians confront this dilemma?

The Catholic Theological Society of USA responded to it on June 6, 1997 with the following resolutions: "There are serious doubts regarding the nature of the authority of the teaching [that the Church's lack of authority to ordain women to the priesthood is a truth that has been infallibly taught and requires the definitive assent of the faithful], and its grounds in Tradition. There is serious, widespread disagreement on this question, not only among theologians, but also within the larger community of the Church . .

It seems clear that further study, discussion and prayer regarding this question by all the members of the Church in accord with their particular gifts and vocations are necessary if the Church is to be guided by the Spirit in remaining faithful to the authentic Tradition." *This resolution was adopted after a secret ballot, with 216 theologians voting 'YES', 22 'NO' and 10 abstaining.*

Elizabeth A. Johnson, C.S.J., professor of theology at Fordham University, New York, wrote: "The reasons [Rome gives] do not hold up, try as one might to entertain them. According to traditional Catholic teaching, the human faculty of judgment is not free, unlike our will. We can give genuine assent only to what presents itself to our mind as true: 'The truth cannot impose itself except by virtue of its own truth, as it makes its entrance into the mind at once quietly and with power' (Vatican II, *Declaration on Religious Freedom*, 1). If a declared teaching or practice continuously jars our mind as missing the mark, as in the present case, it is our responsibility to explore and express the reasons why. This resistance is not to be equated with disloyalty or rebellion, let alone lack of faith, but with a form of loyalty and service." *Commonweal Jan.26, 1996.*

Sr.Joan Chittister OSB one of the speakers at the current Dublin meet wrote: "Can an office of the Vatican declare a papal statement infallible? And can they do it ex post factum? Any time they want to? Maybe hundreds of years rather than months after it was written? Why is it that when bishops all over the world ask for this issue to be discussed, they are simply ignored? When, on the other hand, one of the Vatican congregations addresses the issue unilaterally — even defines its undefined terms — without consultation from the world's body of bishops, let alone the people of God, the subject is happily opened in order to be closed. And without a bishop in sight. Have we come to the point where the bishops of the church are even more ignored than the women of the church?"

Fr. Tissa Balasuriya in his book, *Mary and Human Liberation* says of Mary: "Should she not have been worthy to fulfill the functions of the Christian priesthood such as preside at the Eucharist and share in the teaching of the doctrine of Jesus and administration of the community'? If she was good enough for Bethlehem, Jerusalem, Cana, and Calvary, was she not good enough for (presiding over) the breaking of bread and the sharing of goods'? A well developed Mariology can be one of the best supports for the causes of equality of women and men in the Church at all levels."

Following the Vatican statement a group of 14 sisters from India belonging to a core group self-styled: WORTH (=women Religious Theologising), which had its beginning on Nov.4th 1986 and whose members include lawyers, doctors, theologians, former major superiors, major superiors, spiritual guides and counsellors, also sent a joint dissenting note addressed to Pope John Paul II, on 31st Oct. 1994. In that letter among other things they asked the Holy Father: "When the time had fully come, God sent forth His son, born of a woman..."(Ga.4.4) It was the divine plan to choose a woman to enter into the divine saving act in a unique way. She brought into this world the Incarnate Son of God without the help of a man. How can those who believe in the call of Mary to be the mother of Jesus exclude women from bringing in the Sacramental Presence of Christ in the Eucharist?"

In short the theologians argue that *the Pope's statement does not meet the'Church's own strict criteria for infallibility* and so the present conflict, if any, is to be equated with that of Peter and Paul: "I opposed Cephas [=Peter] to his face since he was manifestly in the wrong . . . I challenged him in front of everyone."Gal.2,11.14. No consultation on the subject has taken place with all the bishops of the Church. Besides an increasing number of the lay faithful believe that women should be ordained. The Holy Spirit is prompting people to continue to discuss and to debate the issue. One should not refuse to interpret and live the Gospel according to the "signs of the times". While women are not to be ordained as an expedient to remedy the shortfall in male

celibate vocations to the priesthood, the shortage of priests throughout the world also may be helping all to discover what God is
doing in and through women. What is urgently needed is for all
Church members to engage in prayerful dialogue – Dublin conference being one clear example — confident that the Spirit will lead
us to the whole Truth.

*   *   *

2

Cross Currents on Dublin Conference

Dr. James Kottoor

What has been the official Vatican view on the Conference theme? How did theologians react to the Vatican View? What has been the thinking of the President of the Republic of Ireland on the subject? What was the make-up or anatomy of the Dublin conference?

Vatican's View on Women Priests

What are the stated views of the Vatican Congregation on the ordination of women to Priesthood? Briefly they can be summed up as follows:

1. Scripture: 1.Jesus Christ did not call any woman to be part of the twelve apostles. His openness to women shows that he did not yield to social opinions of the time 2.Thus he established a permanent norm.3. Even Mary was not invested with the apostolic ministry. 4. Paul excluded women from teaching and presiding in the assembly. This established a permanent norm.

2. Tradition: 1. From the earliest centuries until our time the constant practice of the Church has been *not* to ordain women to the priesthood. The existence of prejudice does not invalidate the fact that the practice constituted Church Tradition. 2. The early ministries of women had no relation to the sacramental priesthood. 3.The Fathers of the Church rejected women priests whenever the question arose. 4. In medieval church law and theology women

were excluded from validly receiving ordination. 5. The doctrine was so firmly settled in later centuries that the Church did not need to publicly defend it.

3.   Theological: The priest acts "in the person of Christ". Since Christ was a man, only a male priest can signify Christ at the Eucharist. 2.In the symbolism of salvation Christ is the Bridegroom and the Church is his Bride. A man should therefore represent Christ in the priestly ministry. The priest's acting in the name of the Church is of less importance. 3 Human rights, such as equal rights for women, do not apply in the context of the ministries. The Spirit does not guide women who believe to have a priestly vocation. For only the Church controls who is called and who is not.

4.   Magisterium: 1. That women cannot be ordained priests has been set forth infallibly by the ordinary and universal Magisterium. 2.The Church has no authority whatsoever to confer priestly ordination on women and this judgment is to be definitively held by all the Church's faithful

Some Theological Musings on wow

Rethinking and self-criticism have become the order of the day in the Church today. As a result some of the earlier beliefs that crumbled in our day are that women are unequal, inferior 'incomplete human beings,' or "defective males"(Aquinas), ritually unclean because of their monthly periods – all cultural prejudices which later became theological prejudices.

In the same way defective were many of the Church's theological thinking on   liberty of conscience, attitude to Jews, crusades, slavery, lending money on interest, torture, the papal states, sex (marital union as carrier of original sin and to be resorted to only for procreation), the view of the Council of Florence in 1442 that all pagans and Jews would certainly go to hell if they did not become Catholics before they died.

The Church did not ordain women, some argue, for the same

reason that for generations US bishops in the South did not ordain black men to serve as diocesan priests, because it was simply unthinkable in the cultural climate of the times. Does the fact that Jesus did not call anyone who was wealthy, or who had not left all his possessions to follow him, bind the Church not to recruit for priesthood from affluent sections? In fact, Jesus specifically forbade his apostles, who are our models for bishops, to live in affluence or to be addressed by pretentious titles. But the church does not teach that she has "no authority whatsoever" to ordain as bishops anyone who is enamored of wealth and prestige. (David Knight)

What the priest at the Eucharist represents is not Christ's male or female gender, but his sacrificial love, his role as mediator. The male-only priesthood is part of a set of skewed values on body, sex and marriage that needs to be reformed. Once people accepted these teachings following the St. Ignatian prescription: "If we wish to proceed securely in all things we must hold fast to the following principle: What seems to me white, I will believe black if the hierarchical church so defines," which today is an insult to intelligence. Cyprian rightly stated long ago: "A custom without truth is nothing else but an ancient error!" (*Letter* 74,9). What is needed today is to correct our flawed thinking and reasoning of the past on many things in the light of new findings.

Ireland's President on Women Priests

What does Mary McAleese the President of the Republic of Ireland who held several distinguished academic posts like Pro-Vice Chancellor, Queen Mary's University Belfast (1994), Director of the Institute of Professional Legal Studies (1987) and Reed Professor of Criminal Law, Trinity College, Dublin (1975) think of Ordination of women?

Taking part in a seminar in Dublin in 1995 on *Women Sharing Fully,* she said: "If I truly believed that Christ was the authority for the proposition that women are to be excluded from priesthood by virtue simply of their gender, I would have to say emphatically that this is a Christ in whose divinity I do not and will not and cannot believe. And that is a very important thing for me to have to say. That is not said lightly. This Christ is too small of mind, too mean of heart to be the Christ of the gospel whom I believe in and whom I know, I like to think, at least as well as the Pope might know Him. He is after all my Father and Mother too."

And writing in *The Tablet, March 15, 1997*, on: It won't Wash with Women she wrote: "The poet, W.B. Yeats, describes the relationships as 'a code of ignoble submission'- a harsh judgment perhaps, given the adverse social status of women across the globe and in virtually every religious denomination in his day. His words, however, find an echo in the more recent words of Pope John Paul II when he said: 'In every time and place our conditioning has been an obstacle to the progress of women. Women's dignity has often been unacknowledged, they have often been relegated to the margins of society and even reduced to servitude ... If objective blame especially in historical contexts has belonged to not just a few members of the church, for this I am truly sorry.' The very fact that this Pope has felt it necessary to return frequently in the past few years to the subject of women, tells its own story. His words are not those of a man who believes he is on the comfortable side of a debate. Far from it; they are the words of a man who is slowly realising that the citadel's defenses have been breached and its once staunch defenders are a declining population.

"Nowadays, when voices are raised in support of a much more radical view of the role of women in the Church, the voices do not come from remote margins or fringes. They are not the test voices of those whose frustrations have driven them out of the Church; they are instead the voices of people (men, women, priests, nuns and the occasional bishop) whose feet and faith are planted four-square inside the Church, who love it, live it and are determined to stay in it and to change it. Anyone attending church-based meetings where the subject of women and the Church is being discussed cannot help but notice, as I have, that the faithful main-stream has changed sides. The conversion process is not yet complete but it is not far from it."

Anatomy of the Conference

Attendance at the Dublin Conference was limited to 500 with advance booking facilities for 300 at the Conference site. Though ecumenical in nature, the conference was organized and spearheaded by Catholics from all over the world. There were 370 participants (320 women, 50 men and an estimated 20 non-Catholics) from 26 countries. Among them were 45 known to be religious or priests. It was mostly a gathering of Catholic laity. Country wise from Ireland there were 102, USA 82, England 67, Germany 20, France 11, Austria, Scotland, Canada, Australia 7 each, Spain, Holland, South Africa 5 each, N. Ireland 4, India, Mexico 3 each, Japan, Portugal, Uganda, Brazil, Belgium 2 each, Kenya, Ghana, Pakistan, Sri Lanka, Switzerland, Denmark and Hungary 1 each. WOW is an ecumenical Organisation of all Christian churches. Since the focus of this conference was women's ordination in the Roman Catholic Church it was heavily loaded with Catholic laity.

The Keynote speaker was an Anglican in the place of Aruna Gnanadason of WCC who had to drop out due to various pressures. Since Vatican had declared the Ordination of women a 'closed issue" the conference did not have the support of the Official Church although the Irish Bishops have not made any public statements about it. According to reliable sources the Vatican authorities were rather embarrassed at the conference taking place and local authorities were powerless to stop it. Humorous comments circulating compared it to cat among pigeons or Child Jesus among Herod's soldiers. The Cardinal-Archbishop of Dublin is a member of the Congregation for the Doctrine of the Faith (CDF) and a friend of Cardinal Ratzinger. So he might not have been too delighted to have the gathering in his diocese!

* * *

3

Why Internationalize Women Priests Issue?

Dr. James Kottoor

One of the speakers at the Dublin Conference on Women's Ordination Worldwide (WOW) was Dr.John Wijngaards, who has done extensive study on the subject and maintains an elaborate website: http://www.womenpriests.org/mrpriest/mpr_tab.htm It provides a long list of articles which appeared in print during the last 10 years and answers questions for and against and presents the state of the discussion today. In an interview the Associated Editor, of *Indian Currents* asked him the following questions and his answers are given below:

1. *Why internationalize the issue of Women Priests in the Catholic Church now, while it is a non-issue for the vast majority of Catholics all over the world, except perhaps for small vocal and affluent sections of the Church in the west?*

Dr.Wijngaards: "A great number of Catholics in Asia and Africa may not be aware of the issue of Women Priests, but that does not mean it is a non-issue for them. The full equality of women in Christ through baptism, including openness to the priestly ministry, is of vital importance to Catholics everywhere. Also in Asia and Africa the Church suffers severely because its priestly ministry lacks the charisms that women would give it. The 80,000 women Religious in India, for instance, provide a valuable service just now, but the ministry of some of them would be greatly enhanced by full participation in the priesthood.

"It is interesting to note in this context that my own research on women priests arose from my experience in India (I was moderator to the CRI Women's section in AP) and from preparatory work I did for the All India Seminar in the NBCLC on "New Ministries in India" (Bangalore 1976). In my paper for that seminar, "The ministry of women and social myth", I urged the Bishops of India to explore the possibility of ordaining women. In 1978 I published: "Did Christ Rule out Women Priests?" (Asian Trading)."

2. *What are the three main issues of Universal appeal (since meant for Catholics) you want to see highlighted, thrashed out and solved at the Dublin conference?*

(a) "We have to raise the level of Catholic adult formation in the faith, so that all the faithful can take part in understanding the true demands of the Gospel and Christ's full vision. In the past - and this applies still to many Catholics in Asia and Africa - the all-male caste of priests were an elite that helped to perpetuate such "myths" as a male predominance wanted by God.

(b) "At present women are allowed by Church Law to a much fuller participation in Church life than is implemented in most local Churches. This should be promoted as a preparation to get the faithful used to women serving as deacons and priests.

(c) "All people who carry responsibility in the Church and who grasp the theological questions, should frankly speak out so that the true picture emerges. At present most theologians and many priests, religious and bishops, also in Asia and Africa, know that the arguments to exclude women from the priesthood are really not valid. Debate on the ordination of women should be free, and not gagged by Church authorities."

3. *What message have you for the numerous religious sisters and dedicated women in India who are too busy with footwashing ministry and have very little time to think about these religious, theological and ecclesiastical luxuries and niceties?*

"My message to them is: 'Wake up!' The priestly ordination of women is not a theological or ecclesiastical nicety, but goes to the very root of our service to people. How will our Catholics, both men and women, understand the full equality of women if they see inequality in our Christian leadership? How will religious women and other Catholic women leaders be able to bring about the necessary changes in the Church's service to the poor, if they are excluded from real authority where it matters? Do not forget that authority in the Church has been made dependent on ordination in Church Law. Last year I visited India and heard again how frustrated many women religious are because of their utter dependence on parish priests and other men who refuse to listen to a woman's perspective. Since there are no valid reasons either from Scripture or Tradition to exclude women from the priesthood, the present exclusion of women from priestly leadership is an unwanted import from medieval anti-women prejudices."

These three questions were put also to the Star speaker of the Dublin Meet, Sr. Joan Chittister who responded saying:

"I will try to answer your questions briefly but sincerely: 1. The fact that a document affecting half the population of the church has been internationally imposed without serious international study and discussion makes this a very important issue, no matter how many people are directly involved with its outcome. It raises questions about the nature of infallibility, the definition of church and the theology of the Holy Spirit which holds that the Holy Spirit works in everyone. In a church that discussed usury, slavery, separation of church and state and the divinity of Jesus for centuries before defining any dogma or doctrine at all in their regard, surely the questions of women deserve at least as much respect. And if not, we ought to be discussing, why not ?

2. Issues of an international nature that the ordination question implies are the nature of God, the nature of priestly ministry and the role of women in the church.

3. The question of the equality, spirituality and role of women in the development of the faith, theology and doctrine is not an "ecclesiastical luxury and nicety." It is of the essence of church, creation, incarnation and baptism. Those women in India who are in foot washing ministries have a wisdom and a truth that is not being heard in any ecclesiastical center, synod or conference in the entire Church. How can our theology be whole if we form it from the experiences of only half the church?

Nobel Peace Prize Laureate

What does Mairead Corrigan Maguire, Nobel Peace Prize Laureate, author of Vision of Peace and co-founder of the Peace People who inaugurated the Dublin conference think of Women Priests?

"Whilst I do not myself feel called to the ordained ministry," Mairead said, " I fully support women who do have such a calling, and hope that the growing movement throughout the world for women's ordination and a renewed priesthood in the catholic church will continue to grow. I do believe that women's ordination in the Catholic Church will happen, and it is only a matter of time."

Asked whether she sees the exclusion of women from priestly ministry as a form of institutional violence, she said: "The argument that women cannot be priests because the Church has always ordained only men, is deeply offensive to women. To be told that because of our 'biological make-up' we cannot be ordained, is a form of spiritual violence being done to women by the Institutional Catholic Church."

What message has she for the hierarchical Catholic Church quite opposed to this new wave? "It is important that the Hierarchical Catholic Church leaders enter into dialogue with those involved in this movement," she thinks and adds: "It is only by compassionate listening to each others stories that we will gain new visions, new perspectives, and a new Pentecost in the Church. Reverence for each person's conscience and calling - particularly women who feel such a calling by God - would be in the spirit of Jesus. We are so culturally conditioned to think of priests as men only, and this has led to a sexist church, which has been deprived of the gifts which women priests could bring to the service of Gods people."

Does the Nobel Peace Prize Laureate have any message for the women in India selflessly involved in the ministry of mercy to the less privileged? "In August 1999 I visited India," she explained, "at the invitation of the Gandhian Movement to launch the Decade for a culture of peace and nonviolence for the Children of the world. I was deeply inspired by the wonderful spirit of the people of India, particularly the women I had the pleasure of meeting. The UN has declared the decade 2001-2010 as the Decade for a Culture of Peace and Nonviolence for the children, and it is hoped that Governments will put peace-education in all schools. The best educators for peace are the parents. "Working for peace means also working for economic justice and human rights for all, based on reverence for life and the environment. I learned much during my visit to India as I witnessed the great spirituality and peaceful co-existence, even in the midst of material poverty. I pray that as India advances technologically its people, will retain their reverence for life, family, community and service to each other, and the Indian women will play an pivotal role in passing on this spirit of peace and nonviolence. I hope too that the Indian Government will halt its nuclear weapons programme and divert the much-needed funds into alleviating poverty and providing for the welfare of its people, as all Governments throughout the world should be doing. I wish the people of India peace and happiness and thank them for what they are doing for peace in the World."

Anglican Rev. Rose Hudson

Rev. Rose Hudson of the Anglican Church gave the Keynote address in the place of Aruna Gnanadason of he WCC. The Associated Editor of Indian Currents asked her: *"Why do you think that the present Roman Catholic practice of not admitting women to priesthood is wrong? As different individuals have different Charismas — to celibate, single or married life — don't you think different institutions or ecclesial formations (churches) have different charismas?"*

Answering this question she said: "I do not wish to comment on this question as I believe that it is really a matter for the Roman Catholic Church. What I do believe however, is that they, for generations, have lost the gifts of women in their midst and will continue to do so until they embrace women as made in the image of God and having the responsibility to fulfill their ministry in orders."

Responding to a second question: *"From your experience in the ordained ministry as a woman priest what are the advantages and disadvantage you have experienced or are experiencing?"* Rev. Hudson answered: "The disadvantages are clearly the prejudices and the failure of the Church to embrace women in ministry along with the gifts they bring. The advantages are clearly the gifts we bring and our different styles of working / functioning. Also the Church will be truly balanced when we have both male and female involvement."

Finally what message has she for women all over the world, especially those in India desirous of dedicated ministry, looking to the outcome of the Dublin meet? "My message to women is to celebrate our womanhood, rejoice that we have been made in the image of God, beautifully and wonderfully. So, do not allow the church to destroy who we are and what we bring," she declared.

* * *

4

Women theologians seek to end Male monopoly

Catholic women theologians in India resolved at their first-ever assembly to find ways to end male dominance in theology and Church decision-making and to bring theology to the people.

"We grapple with constant and persistent marginalisation of women in the Church," said the statement from 23 women including some nuns who met at Pune, 7-8 June 2001. The assembly on "building women's solidarity" decided to form a forum of women theologians to accelerate the development of theology with a women's perspective.

Participants reported being "hurt about the exclusion of the feminist perspective from mainstream theology," meeting organizer Virginia Saldanha, secretary of the Indian Bishops' Commission for Women, told UCA News. They "sought ways to build women's solidarity and to evolve a theology rooted in their lives as Indian women," she said in a brief report.

The meeting statement "strongly" objected to "any attempt to create divisions among women" and to the "exclusion of the feminist perspective from mainstream theology." It also objected to the absence of women in Church policy and decision-making bodies. In their statement the Catholic women also committed themselves to "search for a holistic way of being and becoming" and to network with women of other Churches and religions who have similar commitments.

Saldana, also executive secretary of the Federation of Asian Bishops' Conferences (FABC) Office of Laity, said the meet was inspired by the recommendations of the two FABC Bishops' Institutes for Lay Apostolate on Women and by the specific aims of the Indian Bishops' Commission for women. *UCAN*

Women Priests in the Early Church

Many theologians and Church authorities admit that there is no theological objection to the ordination of women to the priesthood in the Catholic Church. But they contend that it was never the tradition of the Church that in the history of the Church women never presided over the Eucharist

However the following research findings of the eminent theologian, E.S.Schuessler seems to establish that in the early Church women actually presided over the Eucharist on a number of occasions, as a matter of accepted regular procedure:

"The leadership of the community (according to 1 Tim.5.1) consists of male and female presbyters on the one hand, and male and female deacons on the other... The overseer/bishop seems to have been chosen from among the presbyters and as in other contemporary organizations, was primarily the presiding administrator in charge of the collection and distribution of church funds. In this task male and female deacons assisted him. The presbyterium was the administrative council or the committee consisting of the esteemed male and female heads of households." Elisabeth Schuessler Fiorenza, In Memory of Her, Crossroad, New York, 1984, p.290

"Clement testifies that the Valentinians maintained the earliest Christian traditions on prophecy.... Bishop Irenaeus polemicizes against the followers of the Valentinian Marcus. Despite the theological belief system of this group, which contained Gnostic elements, its church order and pneumatic self-understanding seem still similar to those found in 1 Corinthians and Acts. Thus it may be seen to preserve an original apostolic prophetic practice. In this group, every initiate was assumed to have received the direct inspiration of the Holy Spirit.

"Whenever the congregation met, its members drew lots – a traditional Jewish and early Christian practice used to divine the will of God. By means of these lots, they were designated variously for the role of the presbyter, for celebrating the Eucharist as bishop, for reading and expounding the Scriptures, or for teaching or addressing the group as a prophet. All members – women and men – were eligible to act as bishop, presbyter, teacher and prophet. Because these functions changed from meeting to meeting, they never became the exclusive prerogative of particular members. The drawing of lots, and the communal character of Spirit-filled leadership, appears close to what we know about pneumatic worship in the early Christian movements. This practice, moreover, would explain why the New Testament never identifies a presider or leader at the Eucharist, and why non-canonical writings understand prophet as such a Eucharistic leader." E S. Schuessler, idem, p.299. *ICAN*

Women Priests Today

The following words give the existential cry of a Catholic woman theologian, who is a medical doctor and a journalist of wide repute. With regard to the role of women in the Catholic Church, she observes:

"Reflecting one woman's spirituality, (for me) there is no distinction of the sacred and the profane. The life-giving blood of childbirth is intermingled with the life-giving blood of sacrificial death. The words of consecration recall the consummation of the Word made flesh even as they hint at the continuing self-emptying that is women's life. And running through it all is the pain of the womb, of letting go, of exclusion.

"For women this pain is intrinsic to their experience of the Eucharist making it impossible to explore this reality without mentioning the ban on the ordination of woman. This exclusion is a shadowy presence at the Eucharist, setting limits to women's participation in this community meal. For many women it stands, as a counter-witness to Jesus' non-discriminatory table sharing that is without conditions of participation, for it introduces an element of separation – gender...

"In a sacrament that celebrates humanity in all its fullness through the embodiment of the Divine in human flesh, women experience a denial of their humanity, thus making a mockery of the radical union of God and the human."- Astrid Lobo Gajiwala, "The Passion of the Womb: Women Re-Living the Eucharist", in Body, Bread, Blood, ISPCK, Delhi, 2000, p.126

"Woman religious the world over experience the hurt and anger of this exclusion most acutely. They resent having to depend on a stranger for their spiritual nourishment and they are unwilling to be humiliated by priests who use the Eucharist as a weapon of power, withholding it on a whim. They are tired and frustrated by the Church's refusal to recognize their priesthood in the breaking of their bread. Increasingly these women and their lay sisters are creating their own rituals, gathering in Christ's name, sharing bread and wine, using symbols taken out of their knowing and loving. What many of these groups miss, though, is the connection with the universal Church (Susan A.Ross, 1993)." – A L. Gajiwala, idem, p.127.

"It must be said, that women's demand for ordination cannot be reduced to a power struggle. Their exclusion addresses a deeper issue – recognition of their full humanity, not only 'in Christ' but also in all of society and the Church." – A L.Gajiwala, idem, p.130.
ICAN

* * *

5

Some say 'YES' others say 'NO'

Bishops, Rector, Professor, Sisters, Laity

Suresh Pallivathukkal

His Holiness Pope Paul VI in a response to the letter of His Grace the Most Rev.F.D.Coggan, Archbishop of Canterbury, on the Ordination of Women to Priesthood wrote that the exclusion of women from priesthood was in accordance with God's plan for his Church. The Dublin conference has stirred up a hornet's nest. Many look at those holding orthodox views on the subject with loathing, while exponents of priesthood for women with appreciation.

The denial of ministerial priesthood to women is considered by many as the affirmation of male supremacy in the Catholic Church. In this context, the Indian Currents talked to various people from all walks of life and elicited their views on the subject which are revealing.

Bishops' Views

Archbishop Vincent Concessao of Delhi (CBCI Vice President) said the demand for the ordination of women could be due to the sociological factor, where women demand a share in the power struggle. But the power vested with the priests is for service. Yet in a participatory church, the power struggle could be solved if there is an active and full participation from every one. When asked if the option is given by the Church, he said, he would go by the decision of the presbyteries in opening the doors of Delhi Archdiocese to the ordination of women.

Delhi Archbishop, Vincent M.Concessao

The Agra Archbishop, Oswald Gracious, (CBCI Secretary General) taking an uncompromising stand, categorically denied the possibility of ordaining women given the choice by the Church. Even in situations where priests are not available for the administration of sacraments, he prefers to find alternative means other than ordaining women.

Agra Archbishop, Oswald Gracious

The co-adjutor bishop for Meerut Diocese in Uttar Pradesh, Rt.Rev.Oswald Lewis, says we are not the competent people to discuss such a sensitive issue. However, he supports the idea of women deaconate.

Co-adjutor bishop for Meerut Diocese Oswald Lewis

Auxiliary bishop of Delhi, Rt.Rev.Anil Couto

The auxiliary bishop of Delhi, Rt.Rev.Anil Couto, supporting women's ordination in an interview to UCAN prior to his Episcopal Ordination said, "Ordaining women would be a step forward in the full flowering of the Church." But at the same time he is in full support of the teaching of the Church.

Rector, Professor, Nuns

Dr. Kurian Muttathupadam, the Rector of Regional Major Seminary, Jellandhar chooses not to discuss the issue at all as the debate on this has not been encouraged by the Church. He abides by the teachings of the Church.

A professor at the theological faculty who doesn't want to be quoted said, "Do not ask such questions to those in the seminary. We have no opinion! We hold on to the teachings of the Church!!"

In a discussion with a group of religious nuns, we found that many of them hold the view that women should not be deprived of this sacrament. To the hypothetical proposition, if Christ had taken incarnation in our own time, they asserted that he would have chosen women for priesthood. Jesus, who spoke up against the injustices perpetrated on the weak, would surely point his fingers at those who deny the fundamental and sacramental rights of women. But Sr. Dolores, the CRI National Secretary, categorically stated that she was not for the ordination of women.

To a query on whether she would become a priest, given an option, Sr.Selma Pbvm said though she supported the cause, she would not consider herself worthy to be a priest. Sr. Mary Scaria, an advocate, stated that women should have been ordained priests much earlier. She puts forward examples from Bible in support of her view. It was Mary Magdalene who received for the first time, after the resurrection of Jesus, the command to proclaim the message of Good News. As such women are on a strong wicket to argue that they are equally eligible for the priestly ministry and the proclamation of the message of Jesus. She countered the argument that since women were ministering to the needs of Jesus, they should now be content with washing the linen at sacristies and cleansing the parish churches. Women have enough efficiency and talent to become priests. Intellectually they are no less than men. The fatherly/motherly qualities of tenderness and compassion attributed to God the Father and Jesus are more explicit in women. They too are able to keep the confessional secrecy. If the same training is given to women, they will in no way lag behind men in the priestly ministry.

Lay people's Views

Mr. Thomas Antony the chairman jog Delhi charismatic team, does not find any difficulty if women were to celebrate the Holy Eucharist.Mr.Bijoy, a college student, is looking forward to the days when women will sit in the confessional as representatives of Christ. However, Mrs.Sheila, a housewife, is cynical about the Dublin Conference, and she finds it difficult to accept women at the altar celebrating the Holy Eucharist. Miss Mini, a Catholic nurse, says the exclusion of women from priesthood does not mean that they are any lesser in dignity to their counterparts. Even if the Catholic Church decides to ordain women as priests, she feels, the ordinary faithful may find it difficult to accept them, as it is common with any new change.

* * *

6

Indian Sisters' Letter to Pope John Paul II

(The following is the text of the letter which 14 Sisters from India sent on 31ˢᵗ October 1994, in response to Pope John Paul Il's Encyclical, Ordinatio Sacerdotalis excluding Women from Ordained Priesthood in the Roman Catholic Church. ed.)

To: Holy Father John Paul II,
Palazzo Apostolico,
00120 Citta del Vaticano

Subject: Response to the Apostolic Letter of Pope John Paul II on reserving Priestly Ordination to men alone, dated 22 May 1994.

Dear Father,

We are women religious from India, proud of our membership in the Catholic Church and the gift of faith we received in her. We are a movement just five years old. We do not have as yet institutional structure or an office building... We meet once a year to discuss some significant issues in the life of women and in our own experiences and try through theological reflection to deepen our faith and commitment. We write this letter to you with filial confidence that you as the father of all Christian people, will listen to our response to the tone and content of your letter on reserving priestly ordination to men alone (22 May 1994).

1. From our anguished hearts: There are some statements in the latter that are extremely painful for us to read. No.1, Para 2 says, "…her teaching authority which has constantly held that the exclusion of women from priesthood is in accordance with God's plan for the Church." The phrase 'exclusion of women' seems to negate our very membership in the Church. We do have full membership in the Church through the sacraments of initiation namely Baptism, Confirmation and the Eucharist. Then why should we as a class be prevented from certain functions in the Church? Dear Father, who decides what is God's plan for the Church? Is it not the people of God? Do you as the father of this family of faithful exclude us from the people of God even in the common search for God's will for the Church today?

II. God's plan in the fullness of time: "When the time had fully come, God sent forth His Son, born of a woman…"(Gal.4.4) It was the divine plan to choose a woman to enter into the divine saving act in a unique way. She brought into this world the Incarnate Son of God without the help of a man. How can those who believe in the call of May to be the mother of Jesus exclude women from bringing in the Sacramental presence of Christ in the Eucharist? The divine call is gratuitous and how can human decisions bind God not to give a specific call to an entire class of people, in fact half the number of human beings based merely on gender differences?

III. The Sings of the Time – Dialogue:

1. All around us we find different sections of the world community in dialogue with one another. In the political, scientific, economic, cultural and religious fields there are constant dialogue going on for better understanding of others holding different opinions, resolving conflicts and building up mutual respect among groups to make the world a better place to live in. Even in the Church, dialogue among Christian Churches is encouraged. Why the Church does not think of entering into dialogue among its own members?

2. In the Church there are pastoral magisterium, the scientific magisterium composed of scholars who are involved in research,

reflection and writing in Scripture, theology, Church history etc. and the people of God in general. In all these groups the voices of women should be considered as significant especially because it is a group which was and still is continually and systematically suppressed. With the growing consciousness in the world, women are slowly discovering their dignity as children of God and raising their voices.

3. Since 1976 great deal of research, study and writings had been done on the subject of the Church's practice of reserving priestly ordination only to men. Articles and books by scholars showed the intrinsic weakness and inadequacy of the arguments addressed in favour of the official position to exclude women. According to these works, there is no scriptural or theological basis for such an exclusion. All these sincere efforts and hard work by so many men and women of faith and scholarship had been just pushed aside and ignored by this letter. Why dialogue in this matter is so completely denied? In the Church, which is the People of God, ever led by the Spirit towards all the truth (Jn. 16.13), is not dialogue the way to discover Truth?

IV. Legitimising oppression of women:

1. We express our feelings of hurt, pain and humiliation at the fact that this letter completely ignores the struggles of women especially the religious women oppressed by the male clergy. Actually it legitimizes the oppression. The entire sacramental system, jurisdiction, decision-making, administration, in fact every adult function in the life of the Church is in the hands of male clergy. Women are kept forever in total dependency. In plain language, we are relegated to perennial childhood and made to depend on the male clergy for living our Christian religious life. Priests make use of this inequality to their maximum benefit by extracting cheap labour from us. They do not hesitate to put us to moral torture if we do not comply with their unjust demands. Often we, women religious wonder if dedication of our lives to God is only to be the handmaids of celibate priests. They do

not consider us as human persons who need time and necessary means for ourselves to meet our psychological, intellectual and spiritual growth and the freedom to decide our apostolate according to our Constitutions. The fact that our Constitutions are approved by the Holy See has very little meaning because we are just expected to fulfill the demands of the clergy who think we exist merely to do what they tell us. We can give you thousands of examples from our own experience. Do you not see that such oppression is legitimised and perpetuated by this letter? Does the voice of the oppressed within the Church go unheeded?

2. The letter seems to suggest that you have no intention of having any dialogue with us. It is strange that even in this 20th century, men presume that the Divine plan is made known only through them. Are not women, members of the Church? Does not the Spirit dwell in us? How come that the Church symbolised as a woman in the scripture is all male in its official functioning?

V. Making doctrines out of a culture of dominance and subservience:

The occasional praise in the recent encyclicals, of the so-called womanly characteristics do not please us at all. In the name of feminine virtues only servitude and self-negation are praised. The studies in social psychology show that the so called womanly qualities are what the dominant class lay down for the subservient or oppressed class as conditions to win acceptance and appreciation from their oppressors. Since the survival of the oppressed depends on the acceptance by the dominant class, they develop these qualities and train their young ones also in these qualities, establishing them as characteristics of their class. Should the Church see this culture of dominance and oppression as divine ordinance and make doctrine out of it calling it theological anthropology? How can the Church be the mediator of Christ's redemption to all peoples when it keeps half its members (women) in abject subservience and worst type of dependence?

VI. Concocting argument to exclude women: Drawing Mary into this question seems to us that arguments are concocted just to exclude women from priesthood. How could Mary claim priesthood when there was no priesthood during her time? Did Jesus ever claim priesthood? Does not the gospel show us that the Christ-movement was an attempt to liberate people from the dominance of cultic priestly class and lead them to worship the Father in Spirit and in Truth (Jn.4.23)?

VII. Priesthood – instituted by the Church and not by Christ:

1. The letter insists again and again that priesthood was instituted by Christ and that He ordained only men. So the Church has no authority to change it. Is it not a strategy in religions that whatever was instituted by the priestly class was told to people that it originated from God so that people practice it unquestioningly? We have examples in the Old Testament too e.g. the laws in the chapters 21, 22, 23 of Exodus.

2. The words 'Do it in memory of me' are a reference to Yahweh's instruction to Israel to have an annual celebration of the Passover as a memorial of His saving act in liberating Israel from the slavery in Egypt. They were used by Jesus to make His disciples understand that He was instituting a new Passover and a new covenant which would involve not only political liberation as in the Old Testament but the total liberation of the human person. It was an expression of His desire that such a liberative thrust should continue in Christ-movement.

3. During the apostolic times, the imposition of hand (now the main ritual in priestly ordination) was used to impart the spirit to preach the gospel and not to ordain them to priesthood (Acts.9.17; 13.3; 1Tim.4.13-14). In the case of deacons (Acts.6.6), it is clearly stated in the Acts that the apostles said that "it is not right that we should give up preaching the word of God to serve tables. Therefore..." Christ did not ordain priests and there was no priestly class during the New Testament times. Later when the Church

adopted the clerical and hierarchical structure, it absorbed elements of the highly patriarchal Judaic religion from which it originated and the socio-political structures of the Roman Empire where it took root. The Roman Empire had collapsed and it is centuries we had moved away as an independent religion from Judaism. Should we still cling on to those elements which we imbibed from these two realities nineteen centuries ago?

VIII.Conclusion: Dear Father, we love the Church, that is why we are concerned and write to you. In the Vatican documents, frequently the people of God are exhorted to respond to the signs of the times. May we request you to see the signs of the time in the voices of women and what is happening in the other Churches and society? Threatening the Churches that ordination of women is a block to dialogue and union seems to us that the Church prefers to sit in an ivory tower refusing to see the activity of the Spirit in today's global scenario in which dialogue is the mode of interaction, communication and growing together. When women's issues do not even have the dignity to be an object of open dialogue, we feel that our very membership in the Church is negated. We earnestly request you to reconsider the letter and enter into a dialogue with us, women.

Yours sincerely,

Oct.31st , 1994   (14 Indian Sisters with names & addresses)

* * *

Part II

What took place
during
the three-day Conference

7

A Celebration of Women's call to a Renewed Priesthood in the Catholic Church

Mairead Corrigan Maguire

(The Nobel Prize Laureate Mairead Maguire made the inaugural address to the Dublin conference, on June 29, 2001. The statements that made wide publicity in the press were that "this kind of theological argument based on 'biology' is nonsense," that "Vatican's practice of 'silencing' those whose opinions differ.... is an abuse of power... a form of spiritual abuse. It is an assault on the sanctity of a person's conscience, and the removal of the right to freedom of thought and speech." ed.)

My Dear Brothers and Sisters in Christ,

"My soul doth magnify the Lord and my spirit hath rejoiced in God my Saviour." I love these words of the Magnificat. They are the words of a woman who has found inner freedom. A woman who feels fulfilled and whose 'spirit' dances with joy and gratitude to God. Mary says 'yes' to becoming the mother of Jesus, and through the working of the Holy Spirit, the impossible becomes possible.

And just as Mary said 'yes' and gave birth to Jesus, so too each one of us are called to give birth to love and truth. This calling starts in the heart, and for some it may be to an ordained or lay ministry. God chooses whom to call and it comes with our freedom to say 'yes' or 'no'.

And that is why I am so happy to be with you all at this Conference. We come together in celebration of women's call to a renewed priesthood in he Catholic Church. I want to acknowledge my joy at being here in the company of some of these women to whom God has given a priestly vocation. And while I myself, do not feel called to Ordained Ministry, I fully support these women and this Movement.

I want also to thank Women's Ordination Worldwide for their invitation to be present. For a long time, I have believed that woman's ordination in the Catholic Church, will happen, it is only a matter of time. However, before now, I did not feel the need to seek out and listen to women who had such a calling. Now, I have listened and not only will continue to fully support them and this movement, but will do what I can to break down the cold wall of silence and apathy to their plight and pain.

Prior to meeting a woman who explained to me her pain and joy, when she received a priestly vocation, I never much thought about how difficult it must be for women who receive this call from God. We are so culturally conditioned to think of priests as men only. We grow up in a sexist church, which excludes women from ordination.

Catholic theology teaches that priestly ordination is for men only. The Vatican's reasoning for this is that Christ chose his Apostles only from amongst men. They seem to think that maleness is more important than any other attribute, which Jesus possessed. Yet in the Gospels, Jesus' divinity and humanity were more important than his maleness.

But, I believe, once we ourselves break through the cultural conditioning of thinking only of male priesthood, there is no reason why women should not be ordained and very many reasons why they should be ordained. For example, women's ordination is more than Women at the Altar. There is also the serious sacramental element, where women could bring their gifts to help people to understand how the grace of God nourishes our souls through the Sacraments, Scripture and Prayer. Women's ways of nurturing, mediating, meditation, counselling, would help 'feed the human spirit' and would enrich both priesthood and people. However, the most important reason is that our Baptism confirms us as sons and daughters of God and we are all equal in God's sight. In Gen.1.27 we are told that male and female God made them, and that 'in God's own image, they are made'. As the spirit of the Holy Trinity lives in all our hearts so we too share in the divinity of God and are loved equally. Why then does the Vatican not realise how deeply offensive it is to women to be told that because of their 'biological' make-up they cannot be ordained? Many Catholics are coming to see that this kind of theological argument based on 'biology' is nonsense. Moreover, people are coming to realise the spiritual violence being done to men and women's consciences by the Institutional Catholic Church. One Religious sister said it came home to her when she realised she could read the epistle, but not the gospel – we all have our waking moments!

And the spiritual violence is experienced not only by women but also by theologians, priests, religious and laity. We are all aware of the Vatican's practice of 'silencing' those whose opinions differ. In a time when 'Dialogue' is being called for by both secular state, and church bodies, Irish society is permeated with fear amongst clergy and religious, of speaking out on issue such as women's ordination. Indeed they have tragically been forbidden from doing so. Since 1996 when the Pope reaffirmed the Roman Catholic Church's stand on priestly ordination of men only, this was made a doctrine of faith and Theologians and Religious may not speak about this matter. I believe this kind of attempt to control by the Vatican is abuse of power. It is de-humanising, demoralising, and is a form of spiritual abuse. It is an assault on the sanctity of a person's conscience, and the removal of the right to freedom of thought and speech. This kind of spiritual abuse is causing very grave damage to many priests and religious who love their faith, but feel torn between conscience and church rules and regulations. I have met such good people, whose spirit, like a wilted flower, calls out in the words of Gerard Manley Hopkins "Give my Roots Rain…"

I myself give thanks to God for the gift of faith and conscience. Born into a Catholic family, from childhood I have been surrounded with nuns and priests who have blessed me with their friendship. They accompanied me down into the valleys and up onto the mountaintops. I want to publicly thank them today. I have great hope for the Church in the new millennium, and it is because I have met many good shepherds – Bishops, nuns, and priests. I see too many wonderful new forms of discipleship being developed by the laity of all churches, and faiths, but above all, I believe Jesus and take his divine promises very seriously. From time to time also, we see the prophetic church shine through, and the spirit of Jesus comes alive. Such was a time during Vatican II when we heard such sweet words of freedom as 'grace lives in the hearts of all men and women'. We also took great hope from the Council which taught us that we should follow our formed conscience and that our conscience is our most secret core and our sanctuary. I loved this. I undertook a vigorous process of discernment and began to try to inform my conscience, by reading relevant church doctrine, pondering tradition, praying, seeking spiritual guidance and finally taking a decision. However sometimes my decision did not coincide with the Church's teaching! Still, I abided by my decision and did my best not to be disturbed by scruples or guilt. I always asked myself 'what would Jesus do'? And after making my decision, refused to allow man-made traditions to destroy the joy and beauty of my faith in God's presence with me on my journey.

Today the institutional Catholic Church is in the eye of the storm. When the apostles were in the boat and the storm blew up, they were fearful. There is fear and anxiety in the boat today. But there is also hope and joy, because Jesus is present with us on the journey. Jesus and Peter, the fisherman, knew all about storms and boats, exhaustion and disappointments. They knew when it was time to pull the boat ashore turn it upside down, scrape the rubbish and rot off the bottom, repair it, and get back out to sea again. Like the boat, our Church needs renewal. In order to do this can we move out of what one theologian has called 'paternalistic neurosis', that controlling culture within the church which attempts to limit the freedom of people by well-meaning regulations. Many people are rejecting religious authority but hey are passionately looking for religious truth and experience. They can tell the difference between religiosity and spirituality. Can we change the 'power-thinking' that is a throwback to older darker days when the Church vied for wealth, and worldly power? Can we re-discover the beautiful non-violent tradition of Jesus and the early Christians who lived unarmed, loving each other and their enemies? I believe so! I also believe when the Church re-discovers and lives out of its nonviolent roots it will warm people hearts and rekindle their spirits.

Perhaps the time is coming soon for a new Vatican Council, a new Pentecost in the Church? Time to assemble as the people of God, in the spirit of humility and simplicity, and receive the gifts of the Holy Spirit, of happiness, creativity, fulfillment, and freedom. This then is my vision of a renewed priesthood and church. With

Mary, I say 'yes' to this vision, and ask the Holy Spirit 'but how can this be'? Only a deep profound silence comes back to me, the silence of the spirit of truth and love at work in the hearts of all men and women in our world. God's deep peace to you. Deo Gratias.

* * *

8

Keynote Address

Woman Beautifully made in God's Image!

Rev. Rose Hudson-Wilkin

This is indeed, an historic gathering and an historic moment. It reminds me of another historic moment nine years ago. Only then, I was standing in Dean's yard – Nov.11, 1992, Westminster, carrying a poster with the words, *Woman, beautifully and wonderfully made in the image of God,* word I adapted from Psalm 139 which I had read that week, reaffirming for me that I was created in the image of God. That both male and female was part of that special creation and that we were all called to 'represent' Christ.

Let me share something of my journey with you: born and grew up in Montego Bay, Jamaica and baptized as an infant within what was known as the 'Church of England' in Jamaica – later one of our bishops determined 'How can it be the Church of England in Jamaica'. With legislation it became, 'The Anglican/Episcopal Church of Jamaica'. I attended a little mission Church, attached to the St.James Parish Church, Montego Bay. As my faith deepened as a young Christian, I became more and more involved in the life of the church through the Anglican Youth Fellowship – AYF.

At approximately age 14 I had a real sense of being called but had no real way of knowing how this was to be expressed, as there were no immediate female models of ordained ministry. Yes there were women – after all isn't the church full of women – if the women stayed away from the church internationally, the church would be in real crisis. I offered myself to be trained for the Church Army. In 1979 I began that training and returned to Jamica to work. While there I became more acutely aware of the importance of the Sacraments in the life of the Church. But in the very next breath we were told that we could not receive the sacraments because we had no one with male genitalia – my choice of words, not theirs – to consecrate the elements. The city churches were well serviced, but many rural churches were starved of the very elements which were supposed to bring them new life.

That was when really began to engage with the issue provoking others to think and ask themselves questions about women's ministry in all its forms. On returning to live in England, I offered myself for the deaconate. Those in the system wanted to know why I wasn't caring for my husband and one child – so far. It was not a 'Here is someone offering herself for God's ministry and yes! She is a she!!' That was hard to swallow. I persevered and nearly two years later I was accepted in another diocese, no one questioning my legitimacy as a woman – and a black woman – to offer myself to God for that which He has called me.

Today I am the Vicar of two congregations in the East end of London. Along the journey, I have faced rejections along with the welcomes. It's been a double whammy – woman – and black! But what do I do? First, I own the fact that it hurts like hell – no woman for my funeral; they would not want someone black conducting this service; after all it is not really normal to have a black woman. So how do I deal with it? Do I bury my head, get depressed, or worse yet, stay depressed about it? No. After acknowledging my pain, I remind myself that they are the ones missing out – ultimately, it is their loss! – and friends, I do believe this.

At my ordination to the priesthood, I described the experience as that of being pregnant and giving birth. First, there is all that waiting – it is not a passive wait; although the waters burst on that momentous evening in November, it took nearly a year and a half later for the child to be delivered. And it was no easy birth. It was a mixture of pain and joy. Pain because of what we collectively have been through – the women who never made it, who will never become an incumbent, who will be barred from a parish or a particular event, those who will never make it as bishops. Pain for those of us who are constantly told that because of your birth designation you are consigned to a particular place. Pain because of the inability of the whole church to rejoice with us but instead seem to focus on those who are unhappy about this new position.

I am delighted that this is an ecumenical gathering. It reassures me that we are on this journey together. In every denomination there are women who know deep in their hearts that they are being called before God to live out their baptismal call. Yet there are those in authority who are apparently safeguarding the faith – so called gate keepers – who know more than God and who dare to say that they know the will of God – and women play no significant part in that! They fail to remember our Lord calling Martha away from the expected domestic role, to sit, listen and learn, thus being better equipped for the real task of living the faith.

There are those who, with reluctance, say – '*well, I do believe in the ordination of women, but what I can't stand are those women who are strident'*. Strident! What do they mean by this? If by 'strident' they mean articulate women who believe and feel passionately and will express their points of view, then women are strident. Dean Mathews, a member of the Archbishops' Commission in 1935 was in no doubt when he said, "The arguments which have been brought against the eligibility of women to the priesthood are without value"(*The Ministry of Women: Report of the Archbishops' Commission, Church House 1935*). Those who still try to find theological arguments to use are being dishonest. We may be told that we are strident for pressing the Church to keep this issue on its agenda, but we have been the ones who are the true guardians of the faith. We have taught to our children in the homes, in Sunday schools, in campaigning for the General Election in England – the silent voices of women.

Other churches have come to the conviction that ordaining women into the full ministry of the Church is the right way to go. They have gone ahead with the ordination of women, and they are still learning to live together along that journey. No so in the Church of England. We have enshrined in law a division which we may never be able to change. Delegates, I struggle and perhaps we all must struggle as to whether we should have accepted ordination with this condition attached to it. Somewhere deep in my heart I believe the church has begrudgingly obliged us by giving us only part of the carrot – the end bit – instead of the whole carrot. What this means is that some people may never have the privilege of experiencing the gift of a woman priest. What a loss!!

Women, when we get there, we are not going to be the clones of male priests. We are going to be ourselves and we are going to make our offering according to the gifts that God has given to us. What has caused some pain as well is to see intelligent women buying into the myth that women cannot be priests because of some 'accident of birth' – even those themselves who hold high office or are in one of the many professions which once barred them from that position. If we are saying it, then why do we expect the men to be different?

"Our deepest fear is not that we are inadequate. Our deepest fear is that we are powerful beyond measure. It is our light, not our dankness, that most frightens us. We ask ourselves, 'Who am I to be brilliant, talented, fabulous'. Actually, who are you not to be? You are a child of God. Your playing small doesn't serve the world. There's nothing enlightened about shrinking so that other people won't feel insecure around you. We were born to make manifest the glory of God that is within us; it is in everyone. And as we let our own light shine, we unconsciously give other people permission to do the same. As we're liberated from our own fear, our presence automatically liberates others" (Often attributed to Nelson Mandela, but actually by Marianne Williamson)

***

9

Ecumenical Perspective on Women Priests

Church unity or WOW more Important?

Dr. James Kottoor

Aruna Gnanadason

The issue of the ordination of women has been one of the most divisive of issues for the various churches. In 1862, the Order of the Deaconesses was revived in the Anglican Church and Elizabeth Ferrar was ordained as the first deaconess; in 1907, the Anglican Church ordained the first woman, Li Tim Oi a Chinese woman, in Xingxing, in China; the Church of South India started ordaining women 25 years ago and women were ordained in the Church of England for the first time in 1994, according to a privately circulated Paper of Aruna Gnanadason of the Church of South India, a noted Third-world Theologian attached to the Women's Commission of the WCC, who was to deliver the keynote address at the Dublin meet, but could not come for the conference on Women's Ordination Worldwide(WOW)due to various pressures.

Subsequently Rev. Rose Hudson-Wilkin of the Anglican Church was scheduled to give the Keynote address. Gnanadason was to give the ecumenical perspective on Women's Ordination issue to the conference. According to her privately circulated paper which quoting Living Letters says: "There are churches in all regions which forbid the ordination of women, even where they can cite no doctrinal or theological reasons why this should be so. While some churches recognise women's gifts, many are quite slow and even resistant to recognise and support women in ministry. Even where women have – after much struggle – been trained and ordained, fair pay, stable placements and moral support as they exercise their ministry are not guaranteed to them. After graduation many women ministers must wait a long time to receive a posting. They may be forced to choose between vocation and family."

Referring to the Indian situation the paper adds: "In India for instance, many women enter theological schools, as a first choice, fully aware that they have no guarantee of ordination, or even of a job, and even if their churches will ordain them, they have no assurance that local congregations will accept them as priests. They enter anyway, with the conviction that it is their vocation, a call they cannot ignore." Whereas in the Church of England after the first batch of 38 were ordained in 1994, the total number of women's ordination in 1995 rose to "more than 1400, constituting one-tenth of clergy in that church. The Anglicans have observed an increase in religious practice in parishes where a woman priest officiates... the number of parishioners increased by between 10 to 30 percent following the calling of a woman to serve as parish priest."

Church Unity & WOW

How does Women's Ordination issue affect the much sought after goal of Church unity? Gnanadason points to Mary Tanner, former Moderator of the Faith and Order Commission of the WCC (of which the Roman Catholic Church is an official member) who quotes what the Anglican Archbishop William Temple said in 1916: "I would like to see women ordained.... desirable as it would be in itself, the effect might be (probably would be) to put back the re-union of Christendom – and reunion is more important," as the shared view of many committed ecumenists. Therefore "whether the question of the ordination of women can be held responsible for the slow and arduous process to visible unity is a matter of debate" according to her paper.

But the fact is that it did affect unity discussions: " the Anglicans did not join in the United Church of Canada in 1956 because that church ordained women. In the Anglican-Methodist unity scheme in England in the 1960's the Methodists delayed the ordination of women till it was obvious that the unity scheme had failed. Even in the covenanting process that followed involving the United Reformed Church, the Methodists, the Moravian and the Anglican churches, the ordination of women once again was an issue. The Church of England included a separate motion referring to the recognition of women ministers of other churches – this was defeated in the House of Clergy. At the Consultation of united and uniting churches in 1987, the situation was summed up this way: 'For some churches the ordination of women adds to the hindrances to unity; but the united churches are clear that further union for them is being made a more open possibility by the willingness of those to share the ordi-nation of women which they have found to be a creative element in their common life." At the end, the dilemma confronting many churches seems to be the question whether visible church unity is more important than the ordination of women or whether visible church unity is at all achievable unless all baptized members – men and women alike in God's image – can fulfil the ministry to which God has called them in Christ. In the meantime "some have come to maintain that the churches' ministry must include women in order to show to the world the depths of unity in human community and make the gospel and the vision of the kingdom credible in a broken and divided world. The unity of the church ought not to be set over against the unity of the human community."

Not a Feminist Campaign

The Third Assembly of the WCC in New Delhi, in 1961, called on the Working Committee on Faith and Order "to establish a study on the theological, biblical and ecclesiological issues involved in the ordination of women". It came out with the decision that: "Many churches welcome women to the ordained ministry and have found the policy advantageous. Others, having adopted this policy, face serious tensions. In others, the policy is under discussion and provokes heated debate. The matter frequently becomes acute in negotiations for church unity. And even apart from formal negotiations, it affects the mutual relations of churches that ordain women to those that do not. It would be wrong, therefore, to view this issue as a result of feminist demands or agitation by a few enthusiasts. It concerns the total understanding of the ministry of the church and therefore has deep theological significance." This position spoken of nearly 40 years ago remains true till today, according to Gnanadason, though in this period many churches have decided to ordain women to priesthood. "It continues to be regrettable that some churches even today, view this deep longing of women to respond to their vocation as a campaign of a few feminists making unreasonable demands!"

The whole controversy of the ordination of women is also dealt with in two carefully formulated and balanced paragraphs which conclude that: "An increasing number of churches have decided that there is no biblical or theological reason against ordaining women, and many of them have subsequently proceeded to do so. Yet many churches hold that the tradition of the church in this regard must not be changed." This of course satisfies neither the opponents nor proponents of women's ordination.

In any case all these developments are sure to contribute to the proposed Faith and Order, consultation on "Ministry and Ordination in the

Community of Women and Men" to be held in 2002. The decision to hold such a conference was taken by the Faith and Order Board at its meeting held in Toronto, Canada in June 1999. Are we willing to walk together in truth and love in our search for unity? This is the question that accompanies the WCC and its designing of the concept of an "ecumenical space" to provide a safe environment for difficult and church dividing issues, such as the ordination of women, to be discussed." It is therefore hoped that whatever decision an individual church reaches there will be no accusation of heresy but that its decision will be accepted by others as a genuine effort to follow the guidance of the Holy Spirit.

Mysterious Truth

Aruna Gnanadason's paper concludes with the words of Bishop Kallistos Ware, Bishop of Diokleia: "In discussing the ministry of women in the Church, let us not be afraid (as Orthodox) to acknowledge that there is a mystery here which we have scarcely started to explore. In speaking of a 'mystery', I am using the word in its proper theological sense. A mystery is not just an enigma or an unsolved puzzle. It is a truth or a set of truths *revealed* by God to our created intelligence, yet never *exhaustively* revealed because it reaches into the depths of divine infinity. The primal mystery is always the incarnation of Christ (see Ephesians 1:9; Colossians 1:26-27), in which all other mysteries - including the *mysteria* or sacraments of the Church, such as baptism, eucharist and priesthood – find their origin and their fulfilment."

The paper urges all to continue supporting each other in their yearning to be faithful to God's call to ordained priesthood, and to pursue their exploration into being the church by providing "new models of leadership – ready, responsive and courageous; caring, loving and compassionate; inclusive, hospitable and embracing.... so that the Church will be each and every day truly the Church of Jesus Christ. And I say again, we as women, as the Spirit leads us, will pour our ointment on the feet of the church."

* * *

10

Discipleship for a Priestly People!
Preaching Equality & Practicing Inequality?

Dr. James Kottoor *(Reporting from Dublin)*

Sr. Joan Chittister, osb

What is the need of the hour: discipleship or canonical decrees? How to follow Jesus who turned the world upside down, even the religious world of his times? Does discipleship confound "right reason" and "good sense" of patriarchy? Is discipleship an intellectual assent to a body of doctrine? How to distinguish the bogus from the genuine discipleship? Is it membership in a clerical social club called the church, at best designed to comfort the comfortable, instead of coming to grips with a leprous humanity in order to break the chains that bind the poor, the outcast and the disfigured? What does discipleship mean to the fairer half of humanity: to be half disciple, half commissioned, half noticed, half valued? Is discipleship to be reduced to manliness? To remnants of a bad biology theologised? To a theology of inequality and a spirituality of domination in the name of God? Is discipleship denying the right to discuss a festering question — even the infallibility of infallibility — instead of permitting the power of truth to persuade? Can the Church let discipleship die and hope to live?

These were some of the flabbergasting, paradoxical and provocative questions which were greeted with a crescendo of intermittent applause all through out from a rapturous audience at the First international Women's Ordination Worldwide (WOW) meet in Dublin on June 30th, 2001. The speaker was Sr. Joan Chittister, OSB, recipient of 28 honours and awards, the latest being "Honorary Doctorate in Ministry" Catholic Theological Union, on 30 May, 2001. Given below are some of the excerpts from the speech that kept the audience spellbound all through out.

"The question haunts Me: What do the people really need in a period when the sacraments are being lost in a sacramental church?...In diocese after diocese parishes are being merged, closed, turned into sacramental way stations served by retired priests, or married male deacons, both of which are designed to keep the church male, whether it is ministering or not. ... Clearly the Church is changing even while it reasserts its changelessness. It is a far cry from the dynamism of the early church in which Prisca, and Lydia and Thecla, and Phoebe and hundreds of women like them, opened house churches, walked as disciples of Paul, 'constrained, the scripture says, to serve a given region, instructed people in the faith and ministered to the fledgling Christian communities with no apology, no argument, no tricky theological shell games about whether they were ministering 'in persona Christi' or 'in nomine Christi'.

Discipleship, not Decrees

"Clearly, both the question and the answer are clear: what do they really need? They need what they needed when the temple became more important than the torah; they need what they needed when the Faith was more a vision than an institution. They need what they have always needed: they need Christian community, not patriarchal clericalism. They need the sacred, not the sexist. The people need more prophets, not more priests. They need discipleship, not canonical decrees....

"But Christian discipleship is a very dangerous thing. It has put every person who ever accepted it at risk. It made every follower who ever took it seriously on alert for rejection, from Martin of Tours to John Henry Newman, from Mary Mckillup to Dorothy Day. Discipleship cast every fragile new Christian community in tension with the times in which it grew. To be a Christian community meant to defy Roman imperialism, to stretch Judaism, to counter pagan values with Christian ones. It demanded very concrete presence; it took great courage, unending fortitude and clear public posture. Real discipleship meant the rejection of emperor worship, the foreswearing of animal sacrifice, the inclusion of gentiles, the elimination of dietary laws, the disavowal of circumcision — the acceptance of women — and the supplanting of law with love, of nationalism with universalism.

"Then, the following of Christ was not an excursion into the intellectual, the philosophical, the airy-fairy. It was not an arm-wrestling match with a tradition that was more history warped by culture than it was the spirit free of the system. It was real and immediate and cosmic. The problem with Christian discipleship is that instead of simply requiring a kind of academic or ascetic exercise — the implication of most kinds of 'discipleship' — Christian discipleship requires a kind of living that is sure, eventually, to tumble a person from the banquet tables of prestigious boards and the reviewing stands of president, and the processions of ecclesiastical knighthood to the most suspect margins of both Church and society. To follow Jesus, in other words, is to follow the one who turns the world upside down, even the religious world...

Consorting with women

"Following Jesus is a circuitous route that leads always and everywhere to places where a 'nice' person would not go, to moments of integrity we would so much rather do without...To follow Christ is to set about fashioning a world where the standards into which we have been formed become the standards, we too often find, we must ultimately foreswear. Flag and fatherland, profit and power, chauvinism and sexism, clericalism and authoritarianism, done in the name of Christ are not Christian virtues whatever the system that looks to them for legitimacy. Christian discipleship is about living in this world the way that Christ lived in His — touching lepers, raising donkeys from ditches on Sabbath days, questioning the unquestionable and consorting with women.

"Discipleship implies a commitment to leave nets and homes, positions and securities, lordship and legalities to be now — in our own world — what Christ was for His: healer and prophet, voice and heart, call and sign of the God whose design for this world is justice and love. The disciple hears the poor, and ministers to the Hagars of this world who, having been used up by the establishment, are then to find their way alone unaccompanied through a patriarchal world, unnoticed in a patriarchal abandoned world, unwanted in a patriarchal world, but mightily, mightily patronized in a patriarchal world. Discipleship is prepared to fly in the face of a world bent only on maintaining its own ends whatever the cost. The price is a high one. Therese of Avila, John of the Cross and Joan of Arc, were persecuted for opposing the hierarchy itself —and then, later, canonized. Discipleship cost Mary Ward her health, her reputation, and even a Catholic burial. Discipleship cost Martin Luther King his life. To the real disciple, to the true disciple the problem is clear. The church must not only preach the Gospel, but it must not obstruct it. It must be what it says. It must demonstrate what it teaches. It must be judged by its own standards..."

Church on Equality, Slavery

"Religion that preaches the equality of women but does nothing to demonstrate it within its own structures that proclaims an ontology of equality but insists on an ecclesiology of superiority is out of sync with its best self and dangerously close to repeating the theological errors that underlay centuries of church sanctioned slavery...Indeed, Jesus shows us, when women lack jurisdiction, and church commissions lack women and even altar girls are barred in a Christian community that says they are permitted, the invisibility of women in the Church threatens the very nature of the Church. Obviously discipleship is not based on sexism, on civil quietism or on private piety. On the contrary discipleship confounds the 'right reason' and 'good sense' of patriarchy with right relationships and good heart. It pits the holy against the human. It pits the heart of Christ against the heartlessness of an eminently male oriented, male defined, male controlled world....

"The disciple insists, as Jesus did - as the commander Judith did - on a world where women do what heretofore has been acceptable only for men simply because men said so! To the disciple who follows in the shadow of Esther, the savior of her people, the reign of God — the welcome of the outcast, the reverence of the other, the respect for creation — becomes a foreign land made home. 'Come follow me' becomes an anthem of public proclamation from which no one — no one — is excluded and for which no risk is too great. Discipleship, we know from the life of the Christ whom we follow, is not membership in a clerical social club called a Church. That is not an ordination that the truly ordained can abide. Discipleship is not an intellectual exercise of assent to a body of doctrine. Discipleship is an attitude of mind, a quality of soul, a way of living that is not political but which has serious political implications, that may not be officially ecclesiastical but which changes the church that is more ecclesiastical than communal....

Siding with the Poorest

"The disciple takes aim at institutions that call themselves 'free-ing' but which keep half the people of the world in bondage, it takes umbrage at systems that are more bent on keeping 'those kind of people' — improper people, that is — out of them than they are in welcoming all people into them. True discipleship takes the side always, always, always of the poor despite the power of the rich — not because the poor are more virtuous than the rich but because the God of love wills for them what the rich ignore for them. Discipleship cut a reckless path through corporation types like the Pharisees, through system types like the moneychangers and through chauvinist types like the apostles who want to send women away. Discipleship stands bare naked in the middle of the world's marketplace and, in the name of Jesus, cries aloud all the cries of the world until someone, somewhere hears and responds to the poorest of the poor, the lowest of the low, the most outcast of the rejected, anything else — all the pomp, all the gold lace and red silk, all the rituals in the world — the gospels attest, is certainly mediocre and surely bogus discipleship.

"It is one thing, then, for an individual to summon the courage it takes to stand alone in the eye of a storm called 'the real world'. It is another thing entirely to see the church itself be anything less than the living Christ. Why? Because the church of Jesus Christ is not called to priesthood; the church of Christ is called to discipleship. To see a Church of Christ deny the poor and the outcast their due, institute the very systems in itself that it despises in society, is to see no Church at all. It is at best religion reduced to one more social institution designed to comfort the comfortable but not to challenge the chains that bind most of humanity — all of its women — to the cross.

"Women are most of the poor, most of the refugees, most of the uneducated, most of the beaten, most of the rejected of the world. Even in the Church where educated, dedicated, committed women are ignored even in the pronouns of the Mass! Where is the presence of Jesus to the homeless woman, to the beggar woman, to the abandoned woman, to the woman alone, to the woman whose questions, cries and life experience have no place in the systems of the world and no place in the church either...

"What does the theology of discipleship demand here? What does the theology of a priestly people imply here? Women simply half a disciple of Christ? To be half commissioned, half noticed, and half valued?...Before these issues, the footnotes falter, the language serves only to heighten the question, faith itself demands the question. The discipleship of women is the question that is not going to go away...In the woman's question the church is facing one of its most serious challenges to discipleship since the emergence of the slavery question when we argued, too, that slavery was the will of God! The major question facing Christians today, perhaps, is what does discipleship mean in a church that doesn't want women. If discipleship is reduced to maleness, what does that do to the rest of the Christian dispensation. If only men can really live discipleship to the fullest, what is the use of a woman aspiring to be a disciple at all? What does it mean for the women themselves who are faced with rejection, devaluation and a debatable theology based on the remnants of a bad biology theologized. What do we do when a church proclaims the equality of women but builds itself on the structures that assure their inequality?

"When 'tradition' becomes synonymous with 'the system' and maintaining the system becomes more important than maintaining the spirit of the tradition, discipleship shrivels and becomes at best 'obedience' or 'fidelity' to the past but not deep-down commitment to the presence of the living Christ confronting the leprosies of the age... Society called the blind sinful, a female child useless, and a menstruating woman unclean, all of them marginal to the system, condemned to the fringes of life, excluded from the center of the synagogue, barred from the heart of the temple. But Jesus takes each of them to himself, despite the laws, regardless of the cultures, notwithstanding the disapproval of the spiritual notables of the area and fills them with himself and sends them as himself out to the highways and byways of the entire world. To be disciples of Jesus means that we must do the same. There are some things, it seems, that brook no rationalizing for the sake of institutional niceties...

Theology of Inequality

"To say that God is love and not ourselves love as God loves may well be Church but it is not Christianity. To proclaim a theology of equality — to say that all persons are equal in God's sight and at the same time to maintain a theology of inequality, a spiritually of domination in the name of God that says that women have no place in the dominion of the Church and the development of doctrine is to live a lie...How can a church such as this call convincingly to the world in the name of justice to practice a justice it does not practice itself? How is it that the Church can call other institutions to deal with women as full human beings made in the image of God when their humanity is precisely what the church itself holds against them in the name of God? It is a philosophical question of immense proportions. It is the question, which, like slavery brings the church to the test...

"Men who do not take the woman's issue seriously may be priests but they cannot possibly be disciples. They cannot possibly be 'other Christs': not the Christ born of a woman. Not the Christ who commissioned women to preach him, not the Christ who took faculties from a woman at Cana, not the Christ who sent women to preach resurrection to apostles who would not believe it, not the Christ who sent the Holy Spirit on Mary the woman as well as on Peter the man, not the Christ who announced his messiahship as clearly to the Samaritan woman as to the Rock that shattered....

"To most of the world, the colonization of women is as unacceptable now as the colonial oppression of Africa, the crusades against the Turks, the enslavement of the blacks and the decimation of the Indians in the name of God…The humanization of the human race is upon us. The only question for the Church is whether the humanization of the human race will lead as well to the Christianization of the Christian church. Otherwise, discipleship will die and the integrity of the Church with it. We must take discipleship seriously or we shall leave the Church of the future with functionaries but without disciples. The fact is that Christianity lives in Christians, not in books, in documents called 'definite' to hide the fact that they are at best time-bound, not in old errors dignified as 'tradition'. The new fact of life is that discipleship to women and the discipleship of women is key to the discipleship of the rest of the Church.

"The task of the present is not preparation for ordination in a church that either doubts — or fears — the power of the truth to persuade and so denies the right to discuss the festering question of whether or not women can participate in the sacrament of orders…No the task of the present in a time such as this is to use every organization to which we belong to develop the theology of the church to a point of critical mass. We need a group free of mandatums that will organize seminars, hold public debates in the style of the great medieval disputations, hold teach-ins, sponsor publications, write books and gather discussion groups around the topics of the infallibility of infallibility and the 'sensus fidelium'… For as Basho says, we do not seek to follow in the footsteps of those of old. We seek things they sought."

* * *

11

Nuns Defy Vatican's Intimidation!

Interference and intimidation from the part of the Vatican to disrupt the smooth functioning of the First International Conference of Women's Ordination Worldwide (WOW) was one of the themes writ large in the headlines of secular newspapers. The following are some of the headlines that appeared in the Irish Times:

"Delegates to Women priests conference 'intimidated' (29 June), "Vatican accused of the 'spiritual abuse' of women"(30 June), "Nuns defy ban to attend international conference on women's ordination", "Vatican told women priests conference co-ordinator not to attend", "Church 'lives a lie' with equality theology", "Delegates call for abolition of ban on discussion of ordination", " We should think less about women priests and more about the role of the lay person"(2 July).

Three persons on whom pressure was brought upon by the Vatican were Ms Aruna Gnanadason of the World Council of Churches (WCC), an Asian Theologian of the Church of South India, Sr.Joan Chitister, an American Benedictine nun of wide repute as a scholar and writer and Sr.Myra Poole (68) of the Notre Dame Order who lives in London and who was the coordinator of the Conference. The Vatican succeeded to prevent the WCC delegate from attending. Though Ms.Gnanadason, who was to be the keynote speaker she was instructed to withdraw following pressure exerted on the WCC by the Vatican. But she sent her 15-page address for private circulation among the participants and got it reported in the press.

The Benedictine Sister Joan, author of 20 books did not attend the first day but gave her talk on 30 June which was greeted with loud applause throughout. While the Vatican brought pressure upon her through letters, her community of 135 sisters signed a document offering support and another document requesting that, should any sanctions be imposed on her for attending the conference, the same be imposed on them as well. As for Sr. Joan she said: "We survived the Dark ages, feudalism, two world wars. We're not going to let a little letter from Rome get us down," as the congregation had a history of 1500 years.

Sr.Myra Poole the coordinator on the other hand was under great pressure both from the Vatican and from her own congregation. Her superiors reportedly received three strongly worded letters from the Vatican Congregation informing her that she would be dismissed from her Order if she set foot in Dublin. So she was not seen even on the second day morning but took part in the afternoon sessions involving the international panel. The attitude of the Vatican silencing conscientious dissent came under severe criticism already on the very first day from the Nobel Prize winner Ms Mairead Corrigan Maguire who inaugurated the Conference on 28 June. "Why does the Vatican not realise," she asked, "how deeply offensive it is to women to be told that because of their 'biological' make-up they cannot be ordained? Many Catholics are coming to see that this kind of theological argument based on 'biology' is nonsense... We are all aware of the Vatican's practice of 'silencing' those whose opinions differ.

"In a time when 'Dialogue' is being called for by both secular, state, and church bodies, Irish society is permeated with fear, amongst the clergy and religious, of speaking out on issues such as women's ordination. Indeed they have tragically been forbidden from doing so." She called this attempt to control by the Vatican "an abuse of power. It is dehumanising, demoralising, and is a form of spiritual abuse. It is an assault on the sanctity of a person's conscience and the removal of the right to freedom of thought and speech." *(James Kottoor, Reporting from Dublin)*

* * *

12

Discerning the Spirit's New Creation

Dr. John Wijngaards

(Dr. Wijngaards addressed the Conference on June 30, 2001. The text of his speech is given below.)

Thoughts on Strategy

I do not know if you have heard the apocryphal story that the Congregation for Doctrine in Rome met in an emergency session. "We have done everything possible", a monsignore reported, "but many people in the Church *still* believe women can be ordained. We have forbidden all discussion on the topic. We have appointed only bishops who promise not to promote women priests. We make parish priests swear an oath of loyalty. Theologians who speak out are on our black list and are being expelled from their congregations or teaching jobs. It doesn't seem to help."

"We could burn their books!" one consultor proposed.
"We tried. It created the wrong kind of publicity." "We could
ask the Pope to write another encyclical on women", someone
else suggested: "No use. After *Mulieris Dignitatem* two-
thirds of Catholics still think women would make excellent
priests!" "Then we have no other choice", the Prefect of the
Congregation sighed. "We have to stop women from being
baptised!"

Where do we go from here?

Those who oppose the ordination of women usually claim that
the desire for ordination arises from the contemporary drive for
equal rights. They portray the demand for women priests as a
modern and novel idea, a secular invention, the intrusion of profane social equality into the sacred precincts of the liturgy, a giving
in to strident feminist bullying. *Inter Insigniores* blames both
women's emancipation and ecumenical pressure from other
Churches.[1] But while it is true that the climate of social emancipation has helped to raise the question of women's absence from the
ministries, the real origin of the demand lies in our common baptism.

Since Vatican II women theologians have brought a new di-
mension to the Church. They began to systemically expose the
inequality between men and women in all areas of Catholic life: in
worship and spirituality, in the parish and in the home, in theology
as well as in law.[2] They re-examined the roles of women in the
early Church and drew consequences from this for New Testament exegesis.[3] They studied in detail women's lives during various periods of the Church's history.[4] They brought new light, from
a woman's perspective, on matters of liturgical language, imagery
and church symbolism.[5] But none of these women theologians, to
my knowledge, claimed that the equality of women in Christ derives from secular or civil rights. We have to carefully distinguish
between external impulses on a doctrine and its Christian source.

The Second Vatican Council recognised that the Church should pay attention to what modern society is telling us. We should listen to the signs of our times. We are told to "decipher the authentic signs of God's presence and purpose in the happenings, needs and desires which Christians share with other people of our age". [6] The Council endorsed present-day society's concern for equal rights and it singled out the emancipation of women as an important issue. "For in truth", the Council declared, "it must be regretted that fundamental personal rights are still not being universally honoured. Such is the case of women who are denied the right to choose a husband freely, to embrace a state of life or to acquire an education or cultural benefits equal to those available to men." [7] Now it is a fact that the rise of women in society *does* put pressure on the Church. It forces Catholics to answer the question: "Why are women still denied the sacrament of ordination and access to power structures in the Church?"[8] But these wholesome external promptings are not themselves the justification for demanding women's ordination.

That demand comes from our common baptism in Christ. For there is nothing that distinguishes the baptism of a man from that of a woman. As Paul said: "all who are baptised in Christ have put on Christ himself. So there is no difference between men and women ... You are all one in Christ Jesus" (Gal 3, 26-28). Because we do not live any longer in Old Testament times, we do not realise how significant this fact is. The Israelites were God's people, yes, but the men were more God's people than the women. Men did not only dominate in the home and in society. Men enjoyed a privileged status in religion. Only men were circumcised. The covenant was made directly with them. Women belonged to the covenant through their fathers and husbands. The men had to sacrifice in the Temple. The men read the Torah in the synagogues. Women could take part if they wished, but then from a distance. Christ overthrew this fundamental discrimination.[9]

Both men and women equally die with Christ and rise with him to new life. Both men and women become members of his new covenant, and share in his Eucharistic meal on an equal footing. Both men and women in like manner share in Christ's priestly, prophetic and royal dignity. The openness of women to the ordained ministry arises from *within* the sacrament of baptism itself. The cry for social equality may have woken us up. The truth of equality in Christ's covenant has always been there.

The demand for the ordination of women arises from the centre of our Catholic faith. It stems directly from the equality of men and women in Christ's universal priesthood, acquired through baptism. It derives from the nature of the Church as the People of God in which women as much as men are full and equal members. It is implied in women's full participation in the whole sacramental order. It is testified to in the *sense of faith* carried by Catholics who instinctively know that it is not God or Christ who bans women from the priesthood.

There are some important consequences in all this for our strategy. Each of the various groups that together form Women's Ordination Worldwide has already spent much time on planning practical strategies and concrete proposals. I see it as my task to formulate a few important aspects of strategy that may further our common purpose. Without claiming to be exhaustive, I will propose four principles that I trust will lead to fruitful discussion.

Principle One: The movement for the ordination of women needs to position itself squarely in the heart of the Church.

1. The ordination of women priests is part of a much wider reform in the Church. The need of reform does not limit itself to the question of women's ordination. Other linked issues are: pastoral re-shaping of the ministries, lay participation in Church administration, sexual morality (including responsible use of contraception, optional celibacy, re-evaluation of homosexuality), more

co-responsibility on all levels (bishops' conferences, dioceses, parishes), etc. Though the ordination of women is a valid issue in its own right, its effective implementation demands structural reform in many other areas of the Church's life and practice.

2.   The movement addresses all sections of the Church. It is characteristic of a *movement*, in distinction from an association, that it influences society gradually and in all directions, as yeast transforms the dough. All members of God's People: the pope, bishops, priests, religious and the laity, need to re-discover the full equality of men and women in Christ. We will not be satisfied until the whole community of the faithful, led by its pastors, recognises that women should be admitted to holy orders.

3.   The movement aims at transforming the whole Church from within. Full participation of women in all ministries will require an overhaul of church law, of seminary training, ecclesiastical structures, pastoral practices.

4.   The movement should stay squarely within the body of the Church. We should not allow the movement for the ordination of women to be pushed to the fringes, or even: down the cliff, on a rubbish heap outside the Church. This is what our opponents would love to do: to get rid of us as an invasion of aliens, a secular infection, a lump that needs to be amputated.

In other words: we want women to be ordained priests because we are Catholics and we know that opening the priesthood to women agrees with our deepest Catholic convictions. On no account will we allow ourselves to be manoeuvered outside the Catholic community.

I am told that, last century, one of my ancestors in Holland clashed with his parish priest, a disagreement that lasted for 20 years. The reason was that the parish priest levied rent on the seats in the parish church, with the front seats costing more. Sunday after Sunday, my ancestor, Klaas Wijngaards, kept standing up at the back of the church. One day, the PP called out from the pulpit: "For God's sake, Klaas, why don't you come forward and take a seat?" Klaas refused. "Then go home and leave the church!" "I won't", Klaas shouted back. "This is *my* church as much as yours!"

But if we do not want others to push us out, we ourselves should also refrain from doing anything that would put us outside the community of the Church. I refer in particular to arranging for women to be ordained by bishops who are not in communion with the Catholic Church. I am not speaking here of individual women who may discern that in their own case, their priestly vocation weighs heavier than service within the Catholic community. Given the present lack of prospect for ordination in the Catholic Church, I can understand that such women may have valid motives for joining another Sister Church and offering themselves for the ministry there. They should have our full support. But this is quite different from whole organisations or the women's ordination movement *as such* promoting the ordination of women by 'outside bishops'. Such an approach would be wrong for many reasons:

• The hierarchy, however much it needs reform in the way it is organised and in the way it often operates, is part of the sacramental communion of the Church. Christ said about bishops and priests: "Who sees you sees me". We should not destroy the unity of the Church for the sake of an inner-Church reform.

• By going outside the Catholic Church for ordinations, the movement would lose the goodwill of many bishops, priests, religious and lay leaders who, though in silence, are at present on our side.

• We should support the ordination of women by a local Catholic bishop, or Bishops belonging to a national bishops' conference, who in this way build up their own local Church. We have the admirable example of the Czech Bishop Felix Davidek of Brno who ordained women during the communist regime in the 1970s. Bishops are 'vicars of Christ, not vicars of the Roman

Pontiff' and they carry immediate responsibility for their flock 'in their own right'. [10] Of course, they too have to balance the spiritual welfare of their own people against the good of maintaining Church unity. But they might well legitimately decide on scriptural, traditional and theological grounds that, in view of local pastoral needs, the unjustified interference by Roman authorities should be ignored.

● Our purpose is to enable *the whole* Catholic Church to admit women to all ministries. We will have failed if we do not get our reforms incorporated in all structures and levels of the Catholic Church. Leaving the Church does not serve that purpose. At present we experience a serious 'brokenness' in the Church as half its members are excluded from the ordained ministries. But the new 'wholeness' we desire will be achieved rather through a confrontation with the hierarchy, however painful, than through any step that would remove us effectively from the body of the Church.

● It is not our aim to make the priestly ministry possible for a small number of women. We want *all* Catholic women to enjoy the right to full participation in all ministries, including the episcopate and the papacy. This is a more difficult target, but the only one that will do justice to our *Catholic sense*.

The truth will set us free

Campaigners for women's ordination sometimes think that beating the drum of women's rights will bring opponents round - but will it? Do we then not underestimate the power of defense mechanisms? Did the Protestant ridicule of Mary in previous centuries not result in more fervent devotion to her among Catholics? Have we not seen that forced religious attendance in Catholic schools produced youngsters who hated going to Mass? Does external pressure not often generate the opposite effect?

Let us not forget that opposition to women priests is basically a prejudice. As psychological studies have shown, prejudice feeds on its own kind of reasoning. Prejudice justifies its hostility through arguments that pretend to be reasonable. "Prejudice is an emotional rigid attitude that leads one to select certain facts for emphasis, blinding one to other facts."[11] Prejudice bases itself on "selective, obsolete and faulty evidence".[12] The bias against American Africans ('blacks'), for instance, rested on the claim that they were an inferior race, less intelligent, happy-go-lucky, unreliable.[13]

With regard to women as priests, prejudice has ready-made arguments that go back to the Middle Ages. "Jesus did not choose women priests. The Church has never admitted women to holy orders, and-so-on." Arguments used to shore up a prejudice have to be taken seriously because the first step in dismantling a prejudice is for those who hold it to recognise that its basis is false. It requires challenging the truth of one's reasons and one's rationalisations. Overcoming the bias against blacks, for instance, called for a recognition of their intelligence, strength of character and reliability. Bishops, priests or lay people who think it was Jesus who excluded women, should be brought to an awareness of the emptiness of that claim. And their smug assertion that "it was never done" can be demolished by the indisputable evidence that women were admitted to the holy orders of the diaconate through a full sacramental rite of ordination.

The need of a concerted effort to spread correct information follows also from the behaviour of social groups when faced with outside criticism. Remember 'group indoctrination', a phenomenon well known from present-day 'sects and cults' who try to immunise their members by inculcating their own worldview. Throughout the centuries the Church has often acted in a similar fashion. Because of Protestant propaganda and even persecution in some countries, the post-reformation Catholic Church screened itself off as a fortress 'to protect the faithful'. It produced catechisms to counteract attacks by opponents. A similar development is happening now.

Church leaders are well aware of the pressure exerted by women's emancipation in society. Over the past thirty years they have built up an official ideology that tries to spell out 'why the Catholic view is different'. For people who feel insecure in their Catholic identity, the 'official position' is gratefully seized upon. It is not uncommon for women, for instance, to defend the ban against women priests with an appeal to the traditional arguments. [14] They need those arguments to explain to themselves and to others why the Pope is right when he says that the exclusion of women from the ministry is not a denial of their dignity or equal status in the Church. What we should note is that the 'equal rights' argument will not convince such people. Their reaction will be: "So what? This is *not* an equal rights issue. It is Jesus himself who wanted it this way. And he had good reasons." The consequences of all this are clear.

Principle Two. The women's ordination movement needs to sustain a programme of education for change.

1.   Our core members need to be thoroughly briefed so that they can act as facilitators.

It is not enough for our key members to support the ordination of women on the general axiom of 'equality in Christ' (however valid that basic axiom is). They will have to know the arguments for and against.

●   No dialogue with traditionalist members of the Church is possible without understanding *their* way of thinking. Regretfully, facilitators need to be familiar with the main grounds on which women are banned from ordination, and the theological reasons that invalidate these grounds.

●   Facilitators also need to be clear on *positive* reasons from Scripture and Tradition for the ordination of women; and on questions of strategy.

●   The Catholic Internet Library on Women's Ordination already offers a short Internet course on the women priest question that

covers the main areas of debate (http://www.womenpriests.org/
interact/course.htm). It is planning a series of academic courses
with the Federation of Christian Ministries Online Academy (http:/
/www.fcmonlineacademy.org).

Via the media, the general public should be involved in an informed discussion.

We live in a media age and people pick up 'the truth' from the
media. Fortunately, the media are interested in the issue of women's
ordination (they love conflict), but they are liable to overstress the
equal rights angle in the sense of: "The Catholic Church is the last
bastion of male monopolies". While this may be true, it will arouse
defense mechanisms in the minds of many Catholics. It is important, therefore, that the theological arguments also be addressed.

● Documentaries, panel discussions, interviews, in-depth articles
can raise a genuine awareness of the real religious issues that are
at stake and of the flimsy basis for traditionalist claims.

● This needs to be planned with the help of professional media
personnel. Too often we are at the mercy of the media's own
agenda.

2. We need to keep discussion alive among opinion leaders in
the Church.

In the Catholic Church the main opinion leaders are: bishops,
priests, theologians, editors, authors, lecturers and teachers. All
these groups belong to organisations and have regular meetings.
Many of these opinion leaders are sympathetic to the cause of
women priests, but they may need to be prodded to put the issue
on their 'consultation agendas'.

● We must promote seminars, workshops and conferences on
the ordination of women wherever possible.

● Organisations should be asked to devote a regular event (for
instance, their annual meeting) to this topic.

3. Our facilitators could conduct awareness 'courses' on local level.

Most parishes have prayer groups, bible groups, advent or lent groups, women's or men's associations that might be open to such courses.

- A series of meetings (e.g. five evenings) could be organised by a local facilitator during which the issues are presented and discussed. Suitable material for this should be prepared that could include: a small guide, reading matter and accompanying videos.

- Institutions that run theological formation programmes for priests, religious or the laity could offer specific courses on the women priest discussion.

4. Our educational programmes will also inspire confidence.

Struggling against patriarchal structures often seems like fighting for a lost cause. Signs of despondency soon set in. Support is essential, both through proper information and by mutual solidarity. The Church has faced this kind of crisis before, and reforms *have* happened. We can move forward with the firm conviction that what we are working and praying for, will one day become a reality.

Creating contrary experiences

Another lesson we can learn from psychology is that providing correct information is not enough. Prejudice gets its best chance to flourish and grow through what has been called 'social distance'. It is broken down by creating familiarity.

To stay with our previous example of Afro-Americans since the phenomenon was widely studied, people prejudiced against 'blacks' rarely knew them as intimate friends. In this context, psychologists identified six circles of closeness: (1) kinship by marriage; (2) personal friends; (3) neighbours; (4) colleagues at work;

(5) immigrants and (6) visitors to one's country. A research from 1928 showed that standard white Americans would admit white Englishmen or Canadians to circles of family and friendship, would hesitate about Spaniards, Italians and Jews, and would positively bar Negroes, Chinese and Indians. On the other hand, once individuals from these suspect nations *were* admitted to closer circles, prejudice was more easily broken down.[15]

I do not know if you have heard the story about the surgeon who arrived late at the hospital and rushed into the operation theatre where a young man was waiting to undergo emergency surgery. On seeing the patient, the surgeon exclaimed: "He is my son!" The patient opened his eyes and said: "Hi, mum!" — Surprised? We are still not accustomed to think of women as *surgeons*. And what about the young man who said "Hi, mum!" to the bishop?

Familiarity is the key word here. Catholics are used to see only men officiating at the altar, only men taking all decisions in the diocese and the parish. Unconsciously they associate liturgical functions with men. The more they see women in roles that border on the priestly ministry, the more they will overcome inner psychological resistance.

Principle three. The women's ordination movement should promote all developments through which women are given more responsibility in the Church.

In other words: the intermediate steps too count. Psychological barriers have to be broken down by women assuming a more visible presence in the Catholic community.

1.   Women should be at the altar in liturgical settings.

Though the priestly ministry extends much wider than presiding over the Eucharist, it is women's closeness to the Eucharist that will serve as a powerful symbol for traditional Catholics.

• Women already function in Eucharistic worship as members or directors of the choir. This is an advance, since until 1917 women were forbidden to be members of the choir by Church law. This ridiculous prohibition was reiterated more than once by the Sacred Congregation for Liturgy. "Neither girls nor adult women may be members of a church choir" (decree 17 Sept. 1897). "Women should not be part of a choir; they belong to the ranks of the laity. Separate women's choirs too are totally forbidden, except for serious reasons and with permission of the bishop" (decree 22 Nov. 1907). "Any mixed choir of men and women, even if they stand far from the sanctuary, is totally forbidden" (decree 18 Dec. 1908).

In many places women are beginning to function as Mass servers, readers, ministers of Holy Communion, preachers and as presiding over communion services. Here too we have made progress. The 1917 Code of Law restricted all ministries at the altar to males (*CIC* 813). The new Code of 1983 which is still in force today, allows lay people, including women, to be readers, Mass servers, cantors, preachers, leaders of prayer services, ministers of baptism and communion, but only by a 'temporary deputation' (Canon 230, §2-3).

1. Inclusive language should be used at all times during liturgical services. Even if the officiating priest forgets to do this, other ministers such as readers and preachers should observe the rule. People will get the point.

During the prayers of intercession, a regular petition could be inserted asking the Holy Spirit to guide the Church in the matter of the ordination of women, or some such prayer. The formulation has here deliberately to be left open for two reasons: (a) we should not dictate to the Holy Spirit what she should do; (b) all members of the community should be able to join in the petition, whatever side they are on regarding women priests.

2. The movement should encourage all situations in which pastoral authority is entrusted to women.

Present Church law forbids women to be clerics and so deprives all women of clerical offices, which require the power of order or the power of jurisdiction [=church governance] (can. 219, §1 & 274 § 1). On the other hand, Church law allows women to be appointed to many tasks and this should be exploited to the full:

• To be a member of the pastoral council of the diocese (can. 512 § 1) and of the parish (can. 536 § 1).

• To be full members of provincial councils of bishops (can. 443 § 4), diocesan synods (can.463 § 2 & 1.5), the finance committee of the diocese (can. 492 § 1) and of the parish (can. 537).

• To be a financial administrator of the diocese (can. 494).

• To be consultors on the appointment of parish priests (can. 524) and the appointment of bishops (can. 377 § 3).

• To preach in a church or oratory though not the homily (can. 766).

• To be catechists (can. 785) and to give assistance to the parish priest in the catechetical formation of adults, young people and children (can. 776).

• To assist at marriages under certain conditions (c.1112).

• To assist the parish priest in exercising the pastoral care of the community, as parish assistants, or as chaplains in hospitals, colleges, youth centres and social institutions (can. 519).

• To be entrusted with a parish because of a shortage of priests (can. 517 § 2).

• To administer certain sacramentals (can. 1168).

• To hold offices in an ecclesiastical tribunal, such as being judges (can. 1421 § 2), assessors (can. 1424), auditors (can 1428 § 2), promoters of justice and defenders of the marriage bond (can. 1435).

• To hold the diocesan offices of a chancellor or a notary (can. 483 § 2).

- The women's ordination movement should promote the ordination of women as deacons as a first step.

The Church has a well-established tradition of women deacons. It is possible that Rome will make some concession in this regard.

- Women who feel called to the ministry should be encouraged to study full theological courses.

- Suitable candidates should be prepared to serve as deacons. However, the women's ordination movement should never accept a watered-down version of the diaconate for women. If women are ordained deacons, this should be done on the understanding that the sacrament of the diaconate is administered to them as to male deacons.[16]

All the above tasks can be taken up by women under the existing law and the opportunities offered here are not fully utilised. It is encouraging that various bishops' conferences are promoting a better integration of women into leadership roles.[17] At the same time, women are already developing *new* ministries in pastoral settings of North and South America, Africa, Asia and Europe. These may well herald the way in which a reformed priestly ministry will function in the future.

Overcoming organisational control

In recent years Rome has unleashed an unprecedented 'reign of terror' in the Church with the express purpose of suppressing all further discussion on women priests. This springs, no doubt, from the conviction that the ordination of women contradicts Scripture and Tradition, and that the faithful should be spared the ordeal of going through uncertainty and confusion. Powerful measures of organisational control have been put in place and are being constantly monitored.

1. Bishops: Only those men are elected as candidates for the episcopacy who undertake, probably on oath,

● Not to promote the ordination of women. Constant pressure is put on bishops 'to resolutely refuse any support to those people, whether individuals or groups, who defend the priestly ordination of women, whether they do so in the name of progress, human rights, compassion or whatever reason it may be'.[18] Individual bishops receive detailed instructions from Rome regarding supposed 'dissidents' in their dioceses. The Synods of Bishops, which were instituted by the Vatican Council to curb curial monopoly, have been deprived of any real influence by a rigging of the agenda, by saturating committees with members of the Roman Curia, by a subtle censorship of bishops' contributions, by selectively omitting resolutions voted on by the bishops.[19]

Religious Superiors. Whenever a man or woman religious expresses disagreement with Rome's view on women priests, Roman Congregations lean on the Superior General concerned. Usually this happens behind the scenes and religious superiors are urged to keep Rome's intervention secret, but some cases have come out into the open. In October 1994, fourteen prominent Religious Sisters in India belonging to ten different Religious Congregations addressed their objections to *Ordinatio Sacerdotalis* in a letter to the Holy Father. All the Congregations were leaned upon.[20]

1.   Theologians. Professors in seminaries and theological colleges are required to swear the oath of loyalty which now, since *Ad Tuendam Fidem* (28 May 1998),

● Includes agreement to the ban on women priests. Theologians have been dismissed from their teaching posts because of their views on the ordination of women. Others have been warned that they will be dismissed if they speak out on the issue. Rome has issued new instructions that put Catholic Colleges under more direct ecclesiastical control. I know of cases where theologians have been admonished by their bishops, on instigation of Rome, because they had allowed their articles to be published on the women priests' web site. Last year the Bishops' Conference of

England and Wales withdrew sponsorship of a theological conference in Newman College, Birmingham, because I was one of the
speakers.[21]

• Editors, Writers, Publishers. Many Catholic newspapers and
magazines are vulnerable because they are owned by dioceses or
by publishing houses owned by religious congregations. Rome has
issued strict instructions to book censors not to give the *Imprima-
tur* or *Nihil Obstat* to books favourable to women priests. The
Liturgical Press of St. John's Abbey, Minnesota, North American
publisher of *Woman at the Altar* by Lavinia Byrne, allegedly burnt
its stock of 1300 copies when it was informed by the local bishop
that Rome was displeased with the book. A number of Catholic
publishers to whom I showed the manuscript of *The Ordination
of Women in the Catholic Church. Unmasking a Cuckoo's Egg
Tradition*, responded with: "We'd love to publish a book like that,
but we can't in the present climate in the Church!"

• Parish Priests, Lay leaders. Through the new oath of loyalty
priests too are put under pressure to fall in line with Rome's opposition to women priests. The ban to women priests has been incorporated into central Church documents: Church Law (can.
1024), the official Catechism (§ 1577).

• Congresses and Meetings of Catholic Organisations. The
outcome of such consultations is often manipulated by Roman interference. An infamous example is the Third World Congress for
the Lay Apostolate (Rome 1967) that manifested the wide range
of 'hierarchical control mechanisms' that Rome has used ever
since.[22]

The intimidation from above has resulted in a climate in which
many individuals and groups act and speak against their better
knowledge. They feel trapped between conflicting loyalties. On
the one hand, they do not want to disobey authority or risk their
jobs and positions. On the other hand, they realise that Rome's
stand against women priests is really untenable and is doomed to

fail. This becomes a problem of conscience which is 'resolved' with the help of classical rationalisations:

"Authority has spoken. I have to obey." "Everybody else toes the party line. Why should I risk my neck?" "Another Pope will surely change this policy, meanwhile I better comply . . ."

"It is better for the people entrusted to me that I keep my job."

It is not my intention here to condemn the persons who are caught in this terrible dilemma. Their struggle is real. As a professor of Sacred Scripture in the missionary college in London I experienced the same trauma. I continued to teach, saying to myself: "Surely the Church will come round soon! It's better for my students that I stay. I can prepare them for the future ... " That was before *Ad Tuendam Fidem* that imposed the oath. The problem is that, while everyone finds excuses, integrity, truth and credibility suffer. If people comply, and even swear oaths, with bad consciences, the Church itself is gradually being corrupted. For what is more important in theology than that the truth be fearlessly sought out and freely discussed? And what is more important for the teaching authority than that its opinions can be trusted? And what is more dreadful to the People of God than that they are reduced to a bunch of puppets held by a string?

The abuse of power by the Roman Curia calls for an urgent reform of how authority is structured and exercised in the Church.[23] It also calls for special steps on our part.

Principle Four. The movement for the ordination of women should promote integrity at all costs.

5. Pastoral leaders should be encouraged to speak out.

In recent years a number of bishops, religious superiors, parish priests and theologians have spoken out. They deserve our full support and their statements should be widely publicised to encourage others to do the same.

In this context it is useful to remind all concerned that Church functionaries who have sworn the 'oath of loyalty' are not bound by the oath as to parts which go against their conscience. Bishops, for instance, who have promised not to promote the ordination of women as a condition of their admission to the episcopacy, are able to change their position once they realise that the ban against women priests is based on faulty evidence. Bishops know from their study of moral theology that a promise, even if made under oath, ceases to oblige if (a) a substantial error affected their knowledge regarding the object of the promise, or (b) if an error affected the purpose of the promise (e.g. what is good for the Church), or (c) if the promise was made under fear, or (d) if the object of the promise has become impossible or harmful. The promise ceases *ab intrinseco*, as Thomas Aquinas taught: "Whatever would have been an impediment to the making of a promise if it had been present, also lifts the obligation from a promise that has been made."[24]

6. We must 'disrupt the system' by voicing protests on all suitable occasions.

1. It has become clear from many studies that oppressive systems are kept in power through the complicity of silent majorities who disagree, but who allow the oppression to continue.

This applied to the Soviet Union[25] and to dictatorial governments in Latin America,[26and] it has consequences for Christians,[27] also in the context of the women priests' question. Church leaders will continue to ignore the issue unless we constantly remind them of the anomaly. This is known as 'disrupting the system'.[28]

Women's movements in many countries are already engaged in such activity: rallies in front of the diocesan cathedral on regular days; parish priests who refuse to take the oath of loyalty;[29] male

pastoral workers who decline the diaconate until their women colleagues will also be ordained; [30] public billboards demanding 'Ordain Women' and many other actions. The North-American
Women's Ordination Conference is leading the way, and publicising
ideas through its email newsletter *Action Alert* and its quarterly
New Women, New Church. [31]

It is imperative that such demonstrations be stepped up and
maintained.

2. We must expose all forms of behind-the-scene pressure.

Many Catholics would be appalled if they knew how much
pressure Rome is putting on bishops, religious superiors, heads of
colleges, theologians, editors, publishers and writers. Rome often
succeeds because it simultaneously imposes a duty of 'silence'.
No one is supposed to know. But, unless there is a genuine case in
which confidentiality needs to be maintained for some personal
reasons, this secrecy plays into the hands of those who abuse their
power. The answer lies in openness and in revealing publicly what
is happening.

At the Synod on Evangelisation in 1974, Vatican organisers
surreptitiously withdrew a report of what the 200 participating bishops had suggested in their various workshops and substituted it
with a document they themselves had already prepared in advance.
The new document was presented *as if* it was a summary of the
bishops' suggestions. The ploy was only frustrated by some participants courageously unmasking the deceit in a general assembly. [32]

Public awareness in the Church will be aroused if more and
more of such cases are brought out into the light for all to see.

Conclusion

The Catholic Church will eventually ordain women as priests.
How long we will have to wait for this will depend on a number of
factors: the emergence of new leaders, external circumstances such

as the loss of membership and the lack of priests that may force the Church to re-consider its traditional stand, and the degree to which rank-and-file bishops, priests, religious and lay people are willing to challenge the system. But the Holy Spirit should not be underestimated. It has already shown the way in other Christian Churches.

The Catholic Church has gone through crises before. Often the struggles and agonies of its committed members led to revolutionary changes that went even beyond people's hopes and visions. The Spirit wrests new beginnings from suffering and defeat. Old structures need to be knocked down for life to produce new shoots. For our campaign is not just our own, it is the never-ending struggle of the Holy Spirit herself who, in the words of St. Paul, groans in us as we, first-fruits of the Spirit, groan inwardly waiting for our full identities to be set free. And we can be full of hope.

"For the Spirit comes to help us in our weakness. When we cannot find the right words for our prayer, the Spirit herself expresses our plea in a way that could never be put into words. And God, who knows everything in our hearts, knows perfectly well what the Spirit means. For the pleas of the faithful expressed by the Spirit are according to the mind of God."[33]

References:

1. *Inter Insigniores*, 15 October 1976, § 1-4; see also the 'Official Commentary on *Inter Insigniores*', § 1-12, *Acta Apostolicae Sedis* 69 (1977) 98-116.

2. Ida Raming, *The Exclusion of Women from the Priesthood: Divine Law or Sex Discrimination?*, Metuchen 1976; Rosemary Radford Ruether, *The Radical Kingdom. The Western Experience of Messianic Hope*, New York 1970; *Sexism and God-Talk. Toward a Feminist Theology*, Boston 1983; Mary Daly, *Beyond God the Father: Toward a Philosophy of Women's Liberation*, Boston 1973; Elisabeth Schüssler Fiorenza, *Der vergessene Partner*, Düsseldorf 1964; *In Memory of Her*,

New York 1983; *Discipleship of Equals. A Critical Feminist Ecclesia-logy of Liberation*, New York 1993; etc.

3.   Elisabeth Schüssler Fiorenza, *In Memory of Her: Feminist Theologi-cal Reconstruction of Christian Origins*, New York 1983; *Bread not Stone: the Challenge of Feminist Biblical Interpretation*, Boston 1984; *But She Said: Feminist Practices of Biblical Interpretation*, Boston 1992; Karen JoTorjesen, *When Women Were Priests*, New York 1993; Luise Schottroff, *Lydia's Impatient Sisters: A Feminist Social History of Early Christianity*, Louisville 1995; Anne Jensen, *God's Self-Confi-dent Daughters: Early Christianity and the Liberation of Women*, Louisville 1996; Ute E. Eisen, *Amtsträgerinnen im frühen Christentum*, Göttingen 1996; Luise Schottroff, Silvia Schroer and Marie-Therese Wacker, *Feminist Interpretation: The Bible in Women's Perspective*, Mineapolis 1998; etc.

4.   For instance, the *Storia delle Donne in Occidente*, Laterza, Rome 1991, five large volumes, now in many languages; Hulia Bolton Holloway et al. (ed.), *Equally in God's Image - Women in the Middle Ages*, New York 1990; Glenna Matthews, *The Rise of Public Woman: Woman's Power and Woman's Place in the United States 1630-1970*, New York 1992; Susan Hill Lindley, *'You Have Stepped Out of Your Place', A History of Women and Religion in America*, Louisville 1996.

5.   Ann Belford Ulanov, *The Feminine in Jungian Psychology and Chris-tian Theology*, Evanston 1971; *Receiving Woman: Studies in the Psy-chology and Theology of the Feminine*, Philadelphia 1981; Carol Gilligan, *In a Different Voice: Psychological Theory and Women's Development*, Cambridge MA 1982; Charlene Spretnak (ed.), *The Poli-tics of Women's Spirituality*, New York 1982; Virginia Ramey Mollenkott, *The Divine Feminine: the Biblical Imagery of God as Female*, New York 1983; Luce Irigaray, *Speculum of the Other Woman*, Ithaca 1983; Janet Martin Soskice, *Metaphor and Religious Language*, Oxford 1985; (ed.) *After Eve - Women, Theology and the Christian Tradition*, Lon-don 1990; Demeris S. Weir, *Jung and Feminism: Liberating Arche-types*, Boston 1987; Mary Grey, *Redeeming the Dream. Feminism, Redemeption and Christian Tradition*, London 1989; Tina Beattie, *God's Mother, Eve's Advocate. A Gynocentric Refiguration of Marian Symbolism in Engagement with Luce Irigaray*, Bristol 1999; etc.

6.   *Gaudium et Spes*, § 11.

7.   *Gaudium et Spes*, § 29.

8.   Marie-Thérèse Van Lunen Chenu, 'Human Rights in the Church: a

non-right for women in the Church?' in *Human Rights. The Christian contribution*, July 1998.

9. John Wijngaards, *Did Christ Rule out Women Priests?*, Great Wakering 1977, pp. 63-71; see also *The Ordination of Women in the Catholic Church. Unmasking a Cuckoo's Egg Tradition*, Darton, Longman & Todd, London 2001.

10. Vatican II, *Lumen Gentium* § 27.

11. G.E. Simpson and J.M.Yinger, *Racial and Cultural Minorities. An Analysis of Prejudice and Discrimination*, New York 1972, p. 24.

12. M. Macgreil, *Prejudice and Tolerance in Ireland*, Dublin 1977, p. 9.

13. J.W. van der Zanden, *American Minority Relations*, New York 1972. p. 22.

14. Read, for instance, Joanna Bogle, *Does the Church Oppress Women?* Catholic Truth Society, London 1999.

15. E. M. Bogardus, *Immigration and Race Attitudes*, Heath 1928, pp. 13 - 29; see also M. Banton, 'Social Distance: a New Appreciation', *The Sociological Review*, December 1960.

16. The *Maria von Magdala* group in Germany is actively preparing for women's diaconate. Contact: Angelika Fromm, Fritz Kohl Strasse 7, D 55122 Mainz, Germany.

17. (The Netherlands) *Vrouw en Kerk*, Raad voor Kerk en Samenleving, Kaski 1987; 'Oog voor verschil en gelijkwaardigheid', *Kerkelijke Dokumentatie* 4 (1998) no 5, pp. 47-53; (USA) NCCB Committee on Women, 'From Words to Deeds: Continuing Reflections on the Role of Women in the Church', *Origins* 28 (1998) no 20.

18. Letter of the Congregation for Doctrine to Bishops, *Osservatore Romano* 13 September 1983.

19. This has been documented in detail for the Synod on the Family. See J. Grootaers and J. A. Selling, *The 1980 Synod of Bishops On the Role of the Family*, Louvain 1983, 375 pages. Similar manipulations took place at the Synods on Evangelisation, on the Laity, on Africa, on Asia, on Europe, to mention but a few (see *The Tablet*, correspondence 16 Oct - 20 Nov 1999).

20. 'Women Religious in India respond to John Paul II', *Worth* (10 October 1994), Jegamatha Ashram, Ponmalaipatti, Tiruchirapalli 620 004, India.

21. Archbishop Vincent Nichols of Birmingham, prompted by Rome, de-

manded that I undertake in writing not to raise the question of women priests. I refused to do so even though my topic was not directly related to women priests. See *The Tablet*, 24 June 2000, pp. 875-876.

22. J.G.Vaillancourt, *Papal Power. A Study of Vatican Control over Lay Catholic Elites*, Berkeley 1980.

23. B. Tierney, *Origins of Papal Infallibility*, Brill, Leiden 1972; A.B. Hasler, *Wie der Papst unfehlbar wurde*, Munich 1979; P. Chirico, *Infallibility: The Cross roads of Doctrine*, Michael Glazier, Wilmington 1983; J.M.R.Tillard, *The Bishop of Rome*, Michael Glazier, Wilmington 1983; P. Granfield, *The Papacy in Transition*, Gill, Dublin 1981; P. Granfield, *The Limits of the Papacy: Authority and Autonomy in the Church*, Crossroad, New York 1990; L.M.Bermejo, *Infallibility on Trial: Church, Conciliarity and Communion*, Christian Classics, Westminster 1992; H.Küng, *Infallible? An Inquiry*, Collins, London 1971; SCM, London 1994; P. Dentin, *Les privilèges des papes devant l'écriture et l'histoire*, Cerf, Paris 1995; P. Collins, *Papal Power*, Harper Collins, Australia 1997; M. Fiedler & L. Rabben (eds.), *Rome has Spoken...*, Crossroad, New York 1998; E. Stourton, *Absolute Truth*, London 1998; J.Manning, *Is the Pope Catholic?*, Toronto 1999.

24. Thomas Aquinas, *Scriptum super IV libros Sententiarum* dist. 38, q.1, sol. 1 ad 1; D. M. Prümmer, *Manuale Theologiae Moralis*, Freiburg 1936, vol. II, 'De Voto', pp. 326-348.

25. A.D. Sakharov, *Progress, Coexistence and Intellectual Freedom*, Pelican 1968.

26. For instance, G. Gutiérrez, 'Notes for a Theology of Liberation', *Theological Studies* 31 (1970) pp. 243-261; C. Torres, *Revolutionary Priest*, Pelican 1973.

27. H. Gollwitzer, *Veränderungen im Diesseits. Politische Predigten*, Munich 1973.

28. J.B.Metz, *Unterbrechungen. Theologisch-politische Perspektive und Profile*, Gütersloh 1981; R. van Eyden, 'Womenpriests: Keeping Mum or Speaking Out?', (2 November 1996); english text on www.womenpriests.org/teaching/eyden.htm.

29. E. McCarthy, 'Soline Vatinel, the Archbishop and Me', *BASIC Newsletter* (19 January 2000) pp. 26 - 31.

30. In the diocese of Augsburg, Germany; see *Diakonia* 24 (May 1993) nr.3.

31. Both are an absolute *must* for WO campaigners. WOC National Office,

PO Box 2693, Fairfax, VA 22031, USA. Tel. + 1 - 703 - 352 1006. Email: woc@womensordination.org.

32. The details of these machinations were narrated to me, in a personal discussion, by Fr. D. S. Amalorpavadass, one of the two Secretary Generals at the Synod. See *The Tablet*, 6 November 1999, pp. 1506-1507.

33. Romans 8, 26-27.

* * *

13

International Panel Presentation

(On Sunday July 1ˢᵗ, 2001, during an International Panel discussion, leaders of Women's Organisation groups from S.Africa, Uganda, Japan, Hungary and Brazil presented brief reports on developments in their respective countries. A letter of support received from Germany also is added. ed.)

Ordination in South Africa

Velisiwe Mary Mkhwanazi

Dina Cormick & Velisiwe Mkhwanazi launched women's Ordination South Africa (WOSA) on August 9, 1996 in Umlazi & Durban, South Africa.

We began an overt campaign for ordination with public debates and placard signs outside churches. The first debates were very well attended but dropped drastically when the hierarchy pronounced against us. So we soon discovered that Catholics were too nervous and conservative to openly and publicly support us. Since then we limited ourselves to a covert campaign through newsletters!

In general, Catholics in South African are afraid to criticise or challenge Priests, and especially bishops, no matter how they behave. Good examples of this are the stories about priests raping the nuns and similar sex scandals recently exposed in the press. For many of us in Africa it was not news and still people are too scared to discuss these problems. As a result people are losing interest in the Church. They go to church if there is something special like a funeral or wedding, but otherwise they pay little attention to what happens in the church. And then there are an increasing number who wonder why they stay "Catholic". They are angry and frustrated at a lot of hypocrisy.

Our newsletter is proving most successful. Much of the material in it comes from the Internet to which most of our readers do not have access. We share news about what is happening in the rest of the world to encourage our people struggling to find hope in the activities of our international sisters and brothers. So the WOSA newsletter serves as a tool to keep the debate open, to challenge our Catholics to think independently, and to provide a source of information on Catholic views and news around the world. Through the generous funding of The Global Fund For Women (without whom we would not have survived), WOSA newsletters are distributed free twice a year to 450 supporters - including several of our unsupportive hierarchy! We hand them out to anyone who expresses an interest, in the hope we might "convert" or at least open their minds! Our Annual get-together is usually held around March 25 or Mass of Chrism. Public campaigning for women's cause has also led to another round of vindictive personal attacks on several members of the steering committee - but we remain determined not to be intimidated.

A research study conducted by Dina Cormick, in 1995 reveals that South African Catholic women want changes in the institutional church. Most of the women polled were in favour of women priests and married priests. They want equal and full participation in all ministerial roles in the Church. Many of the Catholic women expressed extreme dissatisfaction at the present submissive role of women in the Catholic Church. The overall result is that women on the whole are conscientised and enabled to think independently on hitherto unheard of questions like women's ordination and fairness to the weaker sex.

Uganda Questions Women's Ordination

Mrs. Apollonia Lugemwa

I am sharing with you the views of the Ugandan Catholic women on this question of women's ordination in the universal church. How did discussion on this debate come about in Uganda?

After several decades of massive violation of human rights in Uganda, a radical change came in 1986. The Government came up with a new Constitution in 1995. This Constitution included under Article 34 on specific Women's Rights. Women are assured of full equality with men in all fields. It declares null and void any practice, tradition, cultural custom or law which in any way undermines the equal dignity of women with men. When this Constitution is being taught to people, some do ask whether the refusal by the Catholic Church to accept women priests is not a violation of this section? A similar question is put to Muslims for their support of polygamy, which undermines the basic equality of women with men! This prompts all to seek convincing answers.

For the first time in our history, Uganda has a woman catholic as Vice President of the country, several women Ministers in Cabinet, more than 60 women in Parliament and women District Resident Commissioners who represent the President in Districts and women leaders at all levels of Government. Several women fought in the liberation struggle and some are Majors in the Army. Besides there is a policy of affirmative action to assist women 'catch up' with men in the areas of higher education and in Government and Civil Service. When Catholic Women see the entire opening of new opportunities for them which they never thought about before, they do ask why the Catholic Church cannot also open up for equal opportunities with men.

Since the coming of Christianity to Uganda in the later 1870s both the Anglicans and Catholics have been strongly competing with each other for excellence. Whatever good one Church does, the other also does: whether in building schools, hospitals, orphanage, community development, writing books, opening up new universities and so on. This healthy competition has enabled both churches to be strong so that none can fully outplay the other. Now since 15 years ago the Anglican Church here has allowed women priests. So many Anglican women have taken to the study of theology and become ordained priests. Some are parish priests and some have become Canons. But none as yet has been ordained bishops! When Catholic Women daily see these Anglican ordained women with their 'Roman' collars they begin to ask themselves why their church does not do the same. They fear the Catholic Church may now lose out in the healthy competition with the Anglican Church. Again we cannot easily address this concern without proper education in theology and church history.

In some of our schools bright girls have begun posing questions such as this: 'Tell me madam why should I accept to be Confirmed in a church that discriminates against women, when there are other churches where I can be treated fully as equal to men? Some of these girls may one day enter the numerous new churches where they can be made full pastors and bishops.

One other reason is that within our African traditional religions, women were never discriminated against. There were numerous female deities, female mediums or priests, female diviners and female medicine people. Men of all ranks paid respect to them. The discrimination of women in Christianity seems to have come from the Judeo-European culture but not from the African culture.

When the Catholic Church was first established, the first missionaries appointed many women catechists who did wonderful work. It is only when Congregations for the Religious Sisters were established that the recruitment of women catechists was stopped for a long time. It has resurfaced only after Vatican II but even then it is not much supported by many bishops and clergy.

We African Catholic women leaders need convincing

explanations on these issues so that we can in turn respond to other Catholic women and women in other churches and religions. The questions on which we need a deeper explanation include the following:

1. Is the priestly ordination of women denied on basis of biblical teaching and the fact that Jesus did not have a woman among the Twelve Apostles?

2. Is it denied on basis of Patristic tradition, theological doctrine and teaching? If so, can this teaching be made available in simple language to us?

3. Is it denied simply on the basis of church tradition and discipline? Can we hope for the day when the present restrictions will be removed?

4. Can we as lay women know the reasons why some leaders in the church do not want this controversial issue to be widely debated and discussed?

Knowing that issues of injustice such as slavery and slave trade and the discrimination of black people took such a long time to be condemned by the Catholic Church, is it possible to think that even the ordination of women to priesthood is an issue of injustice based on prejudice and the patriarchal control and vision of the Church?

Until convincing explanations are given on the above questions, it will be very difficult for Catholic women leaders to discuss comfortably the equality of catholic women in the Church. I await your enrichment on this matter.

Women's Ordination in Japan

Naoko Iyori

Japan is a highly male dominated society and maybe our church is more so. We cannot even mention "Women's Ordination" publicly. Women makeup 60% of the catholic population and without us our church cannot survive. Yet often the women are not allowed to take active participation in decision-making or in ministry. We are second-class members.

Some have left the church already because of existing sexism. Others are struggling. But there are also some signs of hope. I have come across a priest who says that the Spirit does not work among men, while the Spirit is so alive and active among women. Also among laypersons there are those who see the need of women priests.

Last year in December we held the Women International Wartime Tribunal in Tokyo. The people listened to the victims of the Japanese military participating in their anger, pain and aspiration for justice. It is the same in the church. We can hear the cries of the wounded and the suffering. They are looking for the tender, compassionate and tolerant face of God the Mother. That is why they need women priests. To realise this, it is important to form solidarity and work in collaboration with our sisters all over the world.

Women's ordination in Hungary

Kornélia Buday
(Doctorate student, Innsbrück, Budapest)

The more recent past of Hungary is well known to all. We belonged to the communist block after the Second World War. The communist regime promised *equality for all*. For women practically it meant a kind of liberation for getting jobs outside of their homes - equally to their husbands - but at the same time they had not been emancipated in their families and households. This *manifold burden and oppression of women* - instead of the promised paradise of liberation – continues to weigh heavily on Hungarian female communities and that is why words like *feminism* or *feminist research* have only pejorative associations in our society.

I have been a teacher when I decided to study theology. My previous naïve images of the church were destroyed as I confronted painful realities. Listening to the lifeless preaching and at the same time facing the suffering of the many outcasts of the church, which is supposed to be acting in the name of Jesus made me confused. I found many divorced and re-married people forbidden to receive Eucharist, married priests and their families full of guilt, humble and devoted women doing their best but are allowed only as sacristan, or cleaner in the church or as teacher of religion in several schools. Priests behaving like kings humiliate them so often. There are the molested victims of paedophilic religious people in single-sex-schools and there is the harmful mysteriousness around homosexuality. The laity are seen as an infants in the eyes of some clerics. All these motivated me to be more aware of what is going on around and within me. My mixed feelings of disappointment, anger, questions, criticism and readiness to fight led me to the theological faculty.

I recognized very soon after the first lectures that theological studies separated from the reality of everyday life would not solve my problems and would not answer my questions properly. I also understood that many of the students were not interested at all in their studies but only wanted to get their degrees. Often there had been a *gap* between the candidates for priesthood and the lay students. The seminarists pass their exams often without any big effort. The very low number of priestly vocations made it necessary to welcome and keep in the seminary all the male applicants even if they are *lacking any serious intention.* After the final exam many of them, both lay and cleric simply leave the church. It is not difficult to lose your faith in such an atmosphere of burnt out, cynical, pessimistic, skeptical professors. Till I got to Dublin to complete my theological studies, I had heard very little about liberation theology or about feminist theological research but rather more about women as the biggest temptation in lectures on the Old Testament. Our biblical scholars were preoccupied most of the time with stories of the bible regarding sexuality or about wives as for instance Mrs. Elisabeth Cow or Mrs. Judy Hen and about their husbands. Lectures on the canon law of marriage were from 30-year-old notes with a massive lack of information of recent theological research.

Those who are disgusted with this ridiculous way of doing theology end up with a sarcastic attitude to life and therefore little interested in priesthood, not even attracted to the church. Although most of the theological students are not against women's ordination, they are indifferent to the whole topic and many of them simply want to be free from the system altogether. Avoiding the feeling of being satisfied with humble female Catholic movements obedient to a male-dominant world that has often nothing progressive and life-giving to offer women, and avoiding a kind of female priesthood imitating the hierarchical structures of male clerics, we need first of all courage to believe in the creative power of the Spirit and to believe in a divine dream that is to be realized in our female selves. Therefore we need to work out new theological approaches. Through systematic study and research we have to show alternatives of new identities to women and men, as well as opening up all the ministries for them, so that *both the blood of Christ and the tears of Mary can be found together and have great importance in the one cup offered at the altar by both women and men.*

Women's Ordination in Brazil
Yury Pueblo Orozco

We are delighted to participate in this conference. I echo the words of Joan Chittister: "True discipleship always takes the side always of the poor and powerless, not because they are more virtuous than the rich, but because the God of Love wills for them what the rich and powerful ignore, debate and refuse for them and their kind."

When speaking of what we in Brazil think of women priests we cannot avoid mentioning the appalling social injustice which exists in our country and which affects women — poor women and black women, in particular. Women are not only excluded from the structures of the Church, but they suffer also because of the consequences of the way the world is organized, of a world structure which the Catholic Church supports.

In Brazil 80% of the population is Catholic and the majority of those who attend Church are women. But, as in the rest of the world, women are excluded from the decision-making process in the Church. At the end of July, the 14th National Eucharistic Congress is to take place.. Two women theologians were invited to write papers. But the Bishops did not accept one of the papers because they considered it contained serious theological errors, and from the second paper they cut off certain polemical passages.

Besides the Church not only restricts women within its own domain but it blocks proposed State Laws meant to promote the rights of women, especially those concerned with sexuality and reproductive rights. With regard to the serious problem of Aids, the Church says 'no' to the use of condoms and preaches abstinence as a form of prevention. "What do they mean by that?" ask the women. Yes, because the Church does not know what goes on in women's lives, in women's beds and in young people's lives it does not see the signs of the times. And still, the church feels it has the authority to speak.

In Latin America, and especially in Brazil, women say: "We do not want to be part of this Church; we are ashamed to belong to this church, but fortunately or unfortunately, we are part of a Catholic culture; we belong to this church and not to some other one." So we consider that it is urgent to fight for a church which is more democratic, just and in solidarity with all its members. The way the church treats women involves issues of human rights and justice. These are the things we have to fight for.

Fighting for social justice and equal rights for women in Church and society are the priorities. We support and we fight along with those women who desire to become priests. That is why we are here today. The most important thing is to construct a discipleship of equals, as in the first Christian community. Not that we want to return to the past, but this is the one great contribution the Church can give to humanity today. We are here today to help oblige the church as a whole to act with justice in the case of women so that a better world may be born.

Letter of support from Germany

Magdalena Bogner
(President of the kfd)

The *Katholische Frauengemeinschaft Deutschlands (kfd)* - the largest community of women in Germany comprising more than 700 000 members is convinced, together with many other women and men of the fact of women's full participation in the complete mission of Jesus and announcing his Gospel teachings. For a long time our organisation has supported the equal participation of women in structures of decision-making as well as in all services and ministries of the So as expressed in the *Leitlinien '99*, of the organisation: *"The Catholic women's organisation of Germany (kfd) supports networks expressing support of the ordination of women in all the common aims."*

Therefore we consider it to be an important task of the Church to discover the charisma of women and their vocation to serve within the church in all spheres of *martyria*, *diakonia* and *liturgia*, so that women entitled by ordination are able to work for the salvation of men and women in our times.

Even today God endows his Church with a large enough number of vocations for the priestly ministry.. The credibility and future of the Church, however, are endangered more than ever if the church does not realize or even refuse these vocations only because women are concerned.

We are happy at the efforts of WOW to get women included in a renewed priesthood in the Catholic Church and we wish the conference in Dublin the reviving and strengthening presence of the divine power so that God's kingdom might grow more and more.

* * *

14

WOW Passes 11 Resolutions

(Drafting of the resolutions at the Dublin meet went through various stages of discussion and scrutiny. Various groups prepared a list of around 20 resolutions. These were taken up one by one in the general assembly where they were regrouped, reworded, voted out or accepted. Some resolutions which could not get 60 per cent of votes were eliminated. That brought down the number to 11.ed)

Preamble: All of us, people of God, have gathered from twenty-six countries and five continents for the inaugural WOW ecumenical conference in Dublin, on 29 June 2001. As followers of Christ we answer the call to radical discipleship and seek justice so that all may participate in the sacrament of orders. The Conference participants hold that vocations are not restricted by gender, race, marital status, sexuality, and educational background or life opportunities.

Resolutions:

1. That this conference calls on the Pope to revoke the ban on the discussion of women's ordination.

2. That this conference calls on each member organisation of WOW to pursue dialogue with local bishops, religious, priests and laity on the subject of women's ordination, in the context of retrieving the discipleship of integrity.

3. That this conference calls on the leaders of the Roman Catholic Church to restore the diaconate to women, as was the practice in the early Church.

4. That this conference encourages women who feel called, to study for the diaconate and the priesthood and resolves to support the establishment of suitable training courses where they were not available to women at present.

5. That this conference resolves to promote the cause of women's ordination by drawing constant public attention to the issue, through regular demonstrations by each member organisation, by an annual world day of prayer for women's ordination on 25 March and by a world conference within three to five years.

6. That this conference calls on ministers in all the churches to adapt the language used in the liturgy to reflect the equal dignity of all God's people. Images of God need to reflect both the female and the male.

7. That this conference salutes Ludmila Javorova, our sister priest, and the women deacons ordained by courageous bishops in the underground Roman Catholic Church in Czechoslovakia and asks that the Vatican join us in recognising the validity of their orders.

8. That this conference proposes that WOW through its member groups create avenues for the financial support of those who lose their position as a result of their stand on the ordination of women.

9. That this conference calls on WOW through its member groups to encourage those women and men who have been punished for their support of women's ordination to tell their story publicly and expose the Vatican's actions.

10. That this conference proposes the setting up of a rapid response email system by WOW in order to support the networking of women's ordination groups.

11. That this conference proposes that the purple stole/ribbon be adopted as the international symbol for women's ordination.

Each of these resolutions were discussed for 25 minutes in the general assembly of 350 participants and passed with a majority vote after incorporating suggested amendments during the discussion.—*(James Kottoor, Rreporting from Dublin)*

* * *

Part III

Aftermath of the Conference

15

Sweet Victory for Nuns who Spoke at WOW

Dr. James Kottoor

WOW's Last Supper includes women, men and children

No noose is good news! No punitive action against the Sisters, who hitherto were seen as defying the Vatican ban. Nay, "The women religious orders are leading the Roman Catholic Church again! These women are truly prophets in the RCC of ours," according to a news release received from Katy Scott of WOC. Why?

Because reports from Vatican spokesman Joaquin Navarro-Valls have confirmed that none of the two Sisters – neither the US

Benedictine Sister Joan Chittister nor the London-based Notre Dame
de Namur Sr. Myra Poole would be punished for taking part in the
Women's Ordination Worldwide meet in Dublin. That made the whole
episode a sweet victory for all women participants from all over the
world from 26 countries in the Conference. In the meantime Soline
Vatinel of BASIC, the spokesperson for the Conference has re-
leased the following statement issued by Sister Christine Vladimiroff,
the Prioress of Sr. Joan Chittister community:

Statement of Clarification

" For the past three months I have been in deliberations with
Vatican officials regarding Sister Joan Chittister's participation in
the Women's Ordination Worldwide Conference, June 29 to 31,
Dublin, Ireland. The Vatican believed her participation to be in
opposition to its decree (Ordinatio Sacerdotalis) that priestly
ordination will never be conferred on women in the Roman Catholic
Church and must therefore not be discussed. The Vatican ordered
me to prohibit Sister Joan from attending the conference where she
is a main speaker.

"I spent many hours discussing the issue with Sister Joan and
traveled to Rome to dialogue about it with Vatican officials. I
sought the advice of bishops, religious leaders, canonists, other
prioresses, and most importantly with my religious community, the
Benedictine Sisters of Erie. I spent many hours in communal and
personal prayer on this matter.

"After much deliberation and prayer, I concluded that I would
decline the request of the Vatican. It is out of the Benedictine, or
monastic tradition of obedience that I formed my decision. There is
a fundamental difference in the understanding of obedience in the
monastic tradition and that which is being used by the Vatican to exert
power and control and prompt a false sense of unity inspired by fear.
Benedictine authority and obedience are achieved through dialogue
between a community member and her prioress in a spirit of co-

responsibility. The role of the prioress in a Benedictine community is to be a guide in the seeking of God. While lived in community, it is the individual member who does the seeking.

"Sister Joan Chittister, who has lived the monastic life with faith and fidelity for fifty years, must make her own decision based on her sense of Church, her monastic profession and her own personal integrity. I cannot be used by the Vatican to deliver an order of silencing.

Scandalizing Faithful

"I do not see her participation in this conference as a source of scandal to the faithful as the Vatican alleges. I think the faithful can be scandalized when honest attempts to discuss questions of import to the church are forbidden. I presented my decision to the community and read the letter that I was sending to the Vatican. 127 members of the 128 eligible members of the Benedictine Sisters of Erie freely supported this decision by signing her name to that letter. Sister Joan addressed the Dublin conference with the blessing of the Benedictine Sisters of Erie.

"My decision should in no way indicate a lack of communion with the Church. I am trying to remain faithful to the role of the 1500-year-old monastic tradition within the larger Church. We trace our tradition to the early Desert Fathers and Mothers of the 4th century who lived on the margin of society in order to be a prayerful and questioning presence to both church and society. Benedictine communities of men and women were never intended to be part of the hierarchical or clerical status of the Church, but to stand apart from this structure and offer a different voice. Only if we do this can we live the gift that we are for the Church. Only in this way can we be faithful to the gift that women have within the Church."

Sr. Myra Poole

According to reports Sr. Myra Poole of Notre Dame de Namur,

the Coordinator of the Conference had initially withdrew from the Conference following pressures brought upon her by the Vatican through her General Moderator, Sr. Ellen Gielty. On further reflection she changed her mind and attended the June 30th session. According to her reported statement she had the full support of her Congregation for her delayed decision to attend the Conference.

A lot of confusion and uncertainty had prevailed during the Conference at various levels in the Church precisely because Pope John Paul 11 had declared in his Encyclical: *Ordinatio Sacerdotalis* of 1994 that ordination of Women as priests in the Catholic Church was a closed question and that it is to be accepted by all the faithful as the teaching of the infallible ordinary magisterium of the Church. And in many countries, especially in the Catholic Ireland, Parish priests and those occupying responsible teaching offices in the Church had to take an oath that they would not utter a word against this papal teaching. Moreover Bishops refused to give any appointment to priests who did not take such an oath. There were several such priest participants who refused to take this oath at the Dublin meet.

When this writer made a courtesy visit to the University Cathedral Parish Priest of Maynooth and was told that he was covering the conference as a journalist from India his first beaming humorous response, half in joke, half in earnest, was: *"Anathama sit"* (you are condemned). From here where do we go? To a new series of discussion for a new discovery of what is meant by the infallible ordinary magisterium of the church, as already hinted at by Sr. Joan Chittister in her speech at the Conference? At the end of it all one is left wondering that there must definitely be a good bit of truth in the paradoxical Church jargon that "one must be first condemned before he is canonized." If that were so it is for anyone to guess, what a long haul it is going to be for Srs. Joan and Myra? We wish them good luck, prophetic vision and courage of their convictions to speak out from housetops following the example of Christ who neither taught anything under the cover of darkness nor silenced any honest questioner!

* * *

16

A Personal Assessment of WOW
Silence Broken, Fear, Shame Banished!

Soline Vatinel

(On July 30ᵗʰ 2001, one month after the Conference, Soline Vatinel, who was the spokesperson at the Conference, wrote the following evaluation. Ed)

It is now one month since the Conference took place. What remains with me is a lasting sense of joy and of gratitude, because we were deeply blessed. I said at the close of the conference that, as organisers, it had exceeded our wildest dreams and I still believe it. In fact even more so now. This is because the conference was meant to be a celebration and it truly was: the photos show so many happy faces!

General view of Dublin Conference in session

Many, before the conference, were wondering what was there to celebrate? The experience of women with a calling to the priesthood had been one filled with so much pain. The church climate had been so hostile and the rejection so crushing that many had lost hope. How could we gather to CELEBRATE women's call to a renewed priesthood? Wouldn't MOURNING be more appropriate? Wasn't meeting a waste of time, another futile exercise in venting one's pain and anger? It could only lead to greater frustration.... Etc. And bitter, angry and dejected people are not much fun to be around, to tell the truth!

Perhaps the real challenge was contained in that invitation to celebrate. Recently a journalist, reflecting on the conference and its aftermath, said to me: "You have started a revolution in the Church!" Time will tell, but what is certain is that to celebrate is truly a revolutionary activity. It stems from the Joy of the Risen Christ, a Joy that nothing and nobody can take away from us .A sign that love is stronger than death.

What some Said

I would just like to relate a few of the comments made to me by some of the participants, which I think are significant. One woman, a religious sister who is a hospital chaplain and who has a vocation to the priesthood, sent a lovely bouquet of flowers to thank us for organizing the conference. She explained what it had meant to her: "When I first came on Friday, I was afraid who might see me there. By Sunday, I didn't care any more, I was no longer afraid."

Another woman said to me: "There was a meeting called for all the women who have a vocation to the priesthood and who were willing to acknowledge it publicly. The amazing thing is that when I got there I found the room was actually too small, so many were there, from so many different countries." And another one, an Irish grand mother in her late seventies sent a thank you card with the words: "I think every woman left the conference with her head held high."

Banished Fear, Shame, Stigma

I believe that the great gift of the conference was that it banished fear. Fear, as Jesus in the Gospel so often reminds us, is the enemy of love. Unfortunately fear has been dominating our Church, as coercion and punishment have been the rule. At the conference, courage shone brightly: I am thinking particularly of the courage of Sr. Joan Chittister, her prioress and sisters, and also Sr. Myra Poole, who had been threatened with severe penalties if they attended. But also the courage of many others, less public, but very real. No longer victims of injustice and exclusion, we found our strength and our dignity.

So the silence was broken, the deadly silence born of fear. "What you have heard in the depth of your heart, proclaim on the rooftops." A voice was given to the priestly call of women; in fact it turned out to be many voices, in many different languages. And it banished the shame and the stigma; for too long women with a vocation to the priesthood had had to hide it, to carry it as a guilty secret. Now it could be brought into the open, affirmed as a godly gift and rejoiced over!

Solidarity replaced Isolation

Coming together from the Four Corners of the earth also broke down the sense of isolation, and the helplessness which goes with it. Women with a calling to the priesthood have so often been made to feel that they are the only one, that there is no support, that they have an individual problem ...At the conference all this was replaced by a wonderful sense of solidarity: Solidarity among women, but also very importantly solidarity among Christians of different denominations and between men and women.

For me the conference was a wonderful experience of being church, of being the Body of Christ. And there was a sense that while we had experienced all the pain of a crucifixion, we now tasted the new life of the Resurrection.

The fruits of this new life are hope and energy, the DYNAMOS of the Spirit: this comes out repeatedly from all the messages we have been receiving since the conference. So many of the participants have gone back with fresh hearts for the journey ahead, emboldened and strengthened .The resolutions for action decided upon at the conference are already being implemented. The good news of the conference is spreading far and wide, bringing hope that change is possible. In fact that change IS already taking place.

NOW IS THE TIME was the rallying call of the conference. Ardent prayer and a discerning reading of the signs of the times had revealed to us that indeed now was the Kairos, the appointed time. We were summoned by the Risen Christ to gather in faith, love and hope. We were richly rewarded by the presence of our ever-faithful God. And our mourning turned into dancing ... MAGNIFICAT!

As I have been reflecting and praying since the conference, two images have come to me to try and grasp the meaning of what we have experienced. One is that of Birth. This image came very strongly to me at the close of the conference and was echoed by another committee member. After a miracle pregnancy, several threatened miscarriages and painful labour pangs we had delivered new life! And then another image has been coming to me equally strongly: that of Pentecost. The presence of the Spirit was so tangible at the conference it left us in awe. We, who organised the conference, know that we did not make it happen. All our hard work was nothing in comparison with the gift we received. A New Church being born? Deo Gratias!

***

Woman why are you weeping?

Discovering Christ in the Tomb of Church!

Dr. James Kottoor

What was the first word of the Risen Lord? "Woman". What were the second, third, fourth and fifth words of the Lord? "Why are you weeping?" They in fact summarized the theme and the mood of the First International Catholic Women's Ordination Worldwide conference in Dublin from June 29 to July 1st. The topic was the place of Women in the Catholic Church today in the context of priestly ministry. Their mood was very near to one of weeping.

Why? "Because they have taken away my (read 'their') Lord. And I (they) don't know where they have put him."Jn.20.13. The women were looking for their Lord in the tomb called the Church for a long time now and they could recognize in those who were managing it only the gardener and not Christ himself or his representatives or any dependable guards. Anguished as though by the scriptural warning: *Qui custodiet ipse custodies* (who will guard the guards themselves) they seemed to be echoing the thoughts of Mary McAleese, the President of the Republic of Ireland: "If I truly believe that Christ was the authority for the proposition that women are to be excluded from priesthood by virtue simply of their gender, I would have to say emphatically that this is a Christ in whose divinity I do not and will not and cannot believe. And that is a very important thing for me to have to say. That is not said lightly. This Christ is too small of mind, too mean of heart to be the Christ of the gospel whom I believe in and whom I know."

Church: tomb or shrine?

Hence they were not fighting but begging prayerfully: "Sir, if you have taken him away, tell me(read 'us') where you have put him, and I(we) will go and remove him."Jn.20.15. All that they wanted to hear from the guardians of the empty tomb called the Church, it seemed, was the endearing beckoning call: "Mary!" Had they heard such a call in unison they all would have responded: "Rabbuni – Master" and would have sprung up to cling on to them with kisses. But they hadn't. Nonetheless they were not exactly kicking at anyone. Manifestly they were frowning at the hierarchical church and making their annoyance felt for being let down. To prevent a repeat of another similar let down the Church has to cease to be a desolate tomb and start being a shrine where Christ's tender humanity is enthroned.

Well, Jesus himself seemed to have made a similar mistake of seeing Mary only as one belonging to the female gender when he called her "woman" thereby wounding her female sensibilities and clouding her vision, which He instantly corrected by calling her by name. This is apparently where the all too male-dominated hierarchical church failed because 'the church never makes mistakes'. The Church men distanced themselves from this conference to the extent of disowning them and refused to take any responsibility for what they were honestly trying to discover at the Dublin Conference. To this writer this is how the conference appeared at its outset — a prayerful but desolate gathering of concerned women trying to discover Christ-like humane treatment in their Church which apparently have become a fossil or an empty tomb without His bodily, lively, vivifying presence. Palpable in the atmosphere of the O'Reilly Conference Hall of Dublin University College at

the inauguration was a pall of gloom that descended on the participants, first because of the bowing out of the Keynote speaker,
Aruna Gnanadason of the Church of South India attached to the
WCC women's commission, reportedly due to severe pressure
brought upon her from certain sections of the Vatican officials,
secondly the absence even of the very organizer of the conference, the London based Sr.Myra Poole of Notre Dame de Namur
herself, at the opening session, and thirdly because of the near
invisibility of the well known elderly scholar, speaker, guide and
leading light in Bendictine spirituality, Sr.Joan Chittister, who though
present was keeping a very low profile, all for fear of the Damocles
sword of just punishment by the Vatican hanging over their heads.
But the atmosphere brightened up with the sudden public appear-
ance of Sr. Joan to deliver her speech at the appointed time on
June 30th morning and the arrival of Sr. Poole in the afternoon to
take part in the International panel discussion.

Composition of the Conference

Though ecumenical in nature, the conference was organized
and spearheaded by Roman Catholics (RC) from all over the world.
There were 370 participants (320 women, 50 men and an estimated 20 non-RCs) from 26 countries. Among them were 45
known to be religious or priests. It was mostly a gathering of RC
laity. Country wise from Ireland there were 102, USA 82, England
67, Germany 20, France 11, Austria 7, Scotland 7, Canada 7,
Australia 7, Spain 5, Holland 5, South Africa 5, N. Ireland 4,
India 3, Mexico 3, Japan 2, Portugal 2, Uganda 2, Brazil 2, Belgium 2, Kenya 1, Ghana 1, Pakistan 1, Sri Lanka 1, Switzerland
1, Denmark 1 and Hungary 1. WOW is an ecumenical Organisation
of all Christian churches. Since the focus of this conference was
women's ordination in the Roman Catholic Church it was heavily
loaded with RC laity.

At the heart of the discussion was not only the papal encyclical
Ordinatio Sacerdotalis of 1994 stating that the Catholic Church

has no authority to confer Priesthood on women but also the clarification issued in 1995 by Cardinal Ratzinger the head of the Congregation for doctrine of Faith that it is part of the infallible teaching of the Ordinary Magisterium of the Church and therefore all the faithful are required to give their definite assent to this teaching and even stop all discussion on it. So the question raised was how could the Church, which defends freedom of conscience and freedom of expression as fundamental rights of every human being deny them to its own members without jeopardizing its credibility. That "truth cannot impose itself except by its own truth, as it makes its entrance into the mind at once quietly and with power"(*Religious freedom, 1*) is also the teaching of the Vatican council. How then can discussion for the sake of clarity and consensus of topics riddled with doubts for thinking minds, be disobedience or rebellion?

To forbid one even to discuss is equivalent to forbidding one to think. Is thought control valid, legitimate and even possible? The machine called mind is installed in every human being, precisely to churn out chains and chains of endless thoughts, ideas and ideals. Every honest idea conceived must be allowed to become flesh in words (just as the *Word was made flesh*) for the benefit of communication and sharing. To arrest it at the conceptional stage is equivalent to legalizing abortion of honest ideas. Can the Catholic Church be promoting abortion of every honest thought? How can one stop thinking and talking about a new book 'Out of the Depths' published quite recently, reportedly narrating the gripping story of Ludmila Javarova, a Roman Catholic woman ordained priest for the underground Church in Czecholovakia during the communist rule?

Especially in this age of globalisaion and communication across boarders at the click of a mouse from your study how can anyone one stop the free flow of ideas, exchange of views and international private or public debates? Just the opposite has happened. Ever since the Church tried to fetter freedom of expression through public oral debates, websites loaded with scientifically documented proofs and arguments tying to demolish the claims of the Vatican stand against the ordination of women in the Catholic Church began to appear. One such is the well documented website: www.womenpriests.org providing solid matter for reading for weeks together. Hence the efforts of the Vatican to ban public discussion have only been clearly counter productive. It was like exerting pressure on the Keynote speaker Aruna Gnanadason to bow out which only gave her added publicity even before she was to address the assembly. Just because she had to withdraw from the meeting her paper was given added private circulaton quite in advance and a weekly like *Indian Currents* got it and published it's substance already on June 25th. In addition the conference participants got the enviable chance of listening to Rev. Rose Hudson an Anglican of Jamaican origin who kept the audience spellbound narrating her adventures and achievements both as a woman priest and black. In fact the spokesperson for the conference thanked the Vatican profusely for forcing the organizers to find a substitute keynote speaker in the person of Rev. Rose Hudson. Just as the forbidden fruit became the most appealing fruit for the Mother of all humanity, whatever was forbidden by the Vatican turned out to be the hot favourite either for public discussion or public attention!

Christ and Questioners

In any case it is hard to digest how anyone can close the mouth of a seeker of truth or honest questioner. Christ never closed the mouth of anyone. There were various types of people who questioned him. Some questioned him just to trap him on the horns of a dilemma. But he told no one to shut up. A person like St.Thomas, the Father of faith for Christians in India, was the most incredulous questioner. His questioning and Christ's response have only helped to confirm us doubly in the belief of the fact of His resurrection. Doubting, questioning and confessing after coming to grips with concrete proof are the normal process a St.Thomas Christian would love to go through and how can any one say that such a thing is *Anathema* in the Catholic Church?

It is only dictators and those who either don't have the answers or are afraid of the questioners resort to silencing their subjects. The Catholic Church is not expected to be a dictatorial set up. Nor need it be afraid of any sort of questioners, as it has survived the dark ages of questioning, conflict and schisms. Even this question of women's ordination is nothing new. It became an organised plea in the Catholic Church already in 1975 when over thousand women raised the issue in Detroit, USA. As they began to get the support of theologians and bishops themselves Vatican tried to silence them with the encyclical in 1994 and a clarifying letter in 1995. This apparently led to the founding of WOW in 1996 as an international organization with Sr.Myra Poole as its first Chair person to coordinate organizations and movements in various countries. Finally it has snowballed into the recently held Dublin meet.

In any case the decision of the Vatican not to impose any punitive action on the Sisters seems to prove the adage that a barking dog seldom bite. So the discussion is bound to go on with or without the blessing of the Catholic Hierarchy. But what the women of the Catholic world would love to see is that their discussions and deliberations are helped to arrive at a consensus under the auspices of the Hierarchy, that they are not addressed as woman belittling their gender, but called Mary recognizing their personality and individuality, so that they can also respond in kind and quality saying: Rabbuni, Master and involve themselves enthusiastically in a ministry of partnership vying to serve (not rule or dominate) one another in preaching, teaching, learning, praying, confessing, forgiving, sanctifying, making the bread and breaking the bread together!

* * *

18

Women's Ordination Opinion Poll Result

Suresh Pallivathukkal

Against the background of Dublin Conference (29th June - Ist July) on the issue of ordination of women in Catholic Church, Indian Currents conducted an Opinion Poll. The response was overwhelming from across the globe. The maximum number of responses were received through e-mail. On the very first day, after the draft of the opinion poll appeared in the Indian currents in the first week of July, the office received 46 responses! Besides e-mail and postal letters our office was flooded with phone calls, many of them appreciating the step taken by Indian Currents in providing a platform to express opinion on a vital issue in the Catholic Church. Kairali TV (a Malayalam - a regional language - TV channel) aired a feature on women's ordination basing on the articles and the opinions expressed in the same issue of Indian Currents.

Our Purpose

We reject outrightly certain allegations against the Indian Currents that it was promoting a partisan view while publishing the articles. Our intention was to help the people think differently. While initiating a discussion on this, we never claimed ourselves to be anti-Church, anti-Pope or anti-sacraments. Our move was purely based on the scripture, tradition of the church and in line with the faith and spirituality of the universal and Apostolic Church. Our intention was neither to politicise the Church nor to transform her into a democracy or mobocracy.

Status of Participants

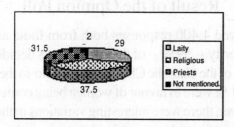

It was quite heartening to see that eleven bishops including three archbishops responded to our query. Among the total number of participants 29% were laity, 37.5% religious, 31.5% priests and 2% did not mention their status.

Method of Response

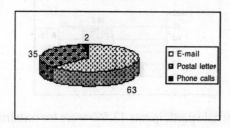

Among the responses we received, 63% were through e-mail, 35 % through postal letters and 2% through phone calls. The urge to respond and react to such an opinion poll reveals that the people of God do not take things lying down. No more are people content with shutting their mouths and say amen to "Roma Locuta, causa finita."

Several of the respondents spoke elaborately on the reason for their choice, even though we hadn't asked to cite any. Many respondents appreciated Indian Currents for what it has been doing for the church in India and for being the voice of the voiceless. A few chose to disagree with the opinion poll and said that since a moratorium is put on the issue, Indian Currents should desist from deviating from its original purpose.

Result of the Opinion Poll

We received 4,400 responses both from India and abroad. While a majority -- 59 % -- of the respondents decided to go by the teachings of the Catholic Church and said 'no' to the ordination of women, 41 % were in favour of women being conferred priesthood. However, there were interesting variations in the way various categories of people responded to the issue. Among the respondents from India, only 23.5 % said that women be ordained while 76.5% were against it. But of the respondents from abroad, the trend was just reverse and 58.5 % favoured ordination of women while 41.5% spoke against it.

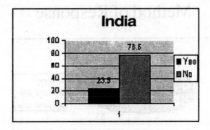

Among the male participants 43.5% were for ordaining women whereas 56.5% were against it. Among the women participants 93% expressed their desire for the ordination of the women, while 7% were against it.

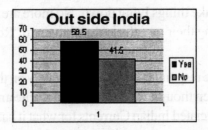

Extracts of the Comments

Arguments were put forward for both Yes and No on the question of the Ordination of Women. Since we had promised to keep the identity of the respondents confidential, we are unable to give more details of the participants. Yet here we have a few excerpts from their views.

Male Participants

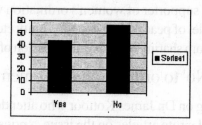

Female Participants

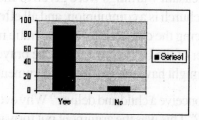

'Yes' to the Ordination of Women

One respondent appreciated Indian Currents for giving vent to the silent desires and longings of many Catholics all over the world and wrote, "God has created male and female in his own image and likeness, therefore, men and women have equal dignity before God as human beings. Since they are equal before God and if men can be ordained, women also can be ordained."

"Women-priests might turn out to be more humane than men-priests."

"Women can be ordained, provided they do not harm the faith of the faithful in Confession."

Another respondent said that there is no theological incompatibility about the Ordination of women. The present rule being a church law, it could be changed. However, the change has to be brought about after a proper and prolonged preparation of the clergy, and the faithful for a change of attitude and removal of prejudices.

A vehement supporter of women's ordination wrote that the church as a model of peace, love, equality, unity etc. couldn't exclude women from sharing in the life and mission of the church.

'No' to ordination of women

Commenting on Dr. James Kottoor who attended the Dublin Conference and wrote articles on the issue, a priest wrote, "I do appreciate Kottoor's writings, but on this issue, I take exception, sorry James." Pleasant warnings were given to Indian Currents and said that the church is a communion, and all efforts have to be made from reducing the church into a democratic institution. Invoking the power of the Holy Spirit someone prayed that Indian Currents family might have the grace of discernment.

"Can a man conceive a child and deliver? Why everybody needs to do everything?" This was the argument put forward by one person against ordaining women. In the garb of fighting communalism Indian Currents is attacking the Catholic Church, another said. Someone wittingly wrote, "Learn the psychology of woman, even before you can think of such a discussion." But one of the best arguments against such a discussion came from a non-Christian and it was published in (8 July issue) Letters to the Editor. " In matters of spirituality and faith, one should not attempt to use the scalpel of reason to dissect belief and established tradition... The right course to adopt is to believe that 'Dad knows best' and leave it at that."

The result may not be indicative of the pulse of the people of God - the Church. It was just a minuscule of the Catholic Church which participated in the poll and the result given here is their way of thinking and not of the whole Catholic Church. We are immensely grateful to all those who have responded to the Opinion Poll, positively or negatively, which made the resultant discussions lively. Perhaps Indian Currents can say that we have once again set the ball rolling.

* * *

19

Letters to the Editor IC

Dad Knows Best!

Sir,

This has reference to Suresh Pallivathukkal's write-up on 'Women Priests' (IC July 10). I wish to draw your attention to what Dr.Kurian Muttathupadam, Rector of Regional Major Seminary, Jallandhar is reported to have told Suresh.

In matters of spirituality and faith, one should not attempt to use the scalpel of reason to dissect belief and established traditions. That way one day, one would kill the very religion on which one's morality and ethics are based. The right course to adopt is to believe that 'Dad knows best' and leave it at that. All devout Catholics should abide by what His Holiness Pope Paul II advises and directs and free themselves of all doubts. Very rightly Dr.Kurian has said that he would abide by the teachings of the Church. And I, with that all the followers of all religions, could say 'abide by the teachings of their respective orders'.

S.P. Banerjee, IPS'

WOW and IC Tie up?

Sir,

IC of 1st July 2001 dedicates almost 16 pages and the present issue still more, to the issue of women priests. Is it that the IC is finding it difficult to get relevant topics or articles? I am a resident in the Western Europe since l994 and I feel you are not in touch with the reality in Europe. It is absolutely a non-issue. The Dublin conference of W.O.W, of which you are speaking so elaborately and profusely, don't get any coverage in the standard visual-audio-print media here – may be with the exception of the organs of the interested parties.

Fr. James Pereppadan, Rome

Sweet Victory for Nuns

Sir,

Just read Dr.Kottoor's write-ups. Especially I loved his reporting on Sweet Victory for Nuns and the specific Benedictine charism within the cathloic church. Most people think that the religious are a sort of emasculated peons of the Vatican beauracracy.

They ignore the special call of the orders and that disorderly thinking and its aftermath are devastating to the church at large and the world in which the church is to function as salt and leaven. You remind the readers that religious call is something different, by quoting the statement of Sr. Vladimiroff osb.

Alphonse Bernard, New York (on e-mail)

Dream of Equality

Sir,

"Women Priests in Catholic Church" (IC, 1 July 2001) is very enlightening. After going through the article through and through, I changed my thinking from not ordaining women to ordaining them in the Catholic Church. Especially Mary's priestly role was so striking and provocative.

Right from the annunciation to the death of her son Jesus on Calvary, she played a powerful role as a priest and became the Mother of Priests. In the ecclesiastical journey of the Church from time immemorial there were sign-posts and stops in reforming, re-thinking, re-planning and in self-criticizing in the journey forward. Now this issue on women priests in the Catholic Church is only a step forward, to stop and to go further effectively.

Jesus Christ who stood against the then social, political, cultural, religious ethos of Palestine, continues to stand against the current discriminating society. Luke's gospel, the gospel of women, is a gem in advocating the uplifting of the weaker sections, especially of women. Now the Church should continue to be a gospel in this mission. Citing from scripture, Gen: 2:22 speaks of God creating woman from the rib of man. Theologically speaking it symbolizes equality between man and woman. The statement of St. Paul in Gal 3:27 "All baptised in Christ, you have all clothed yourselves in Christ, and there are no more distinctions between Jew and Greek slave and free, male and female, but all of you are one in Christ Jesus," is cited to remove all forms of discrimination based on sex. And I Peter 2:9 also highlights the priesthood extended to all the baptized, both men and women.

Now is the time to break the tradition rather than to pull on with it. The Holy Spirit is working with the sensus fidelium in promoting women's ordination. Let us all continue to dream of the day when the man priest and the woman priest would stand before the altar, without any discrimination, sharing in the one priesthood of Christ, as a symbol of equality, to be a model for society.

Bro. Kirankumar Medipally, Chennai

Struggle for Equality?

Sir,

Though the topic "Women Priesthood" is a very lively one in the Church, still I consider it outdated. The reason is that I do not find any progress in the arguments and counter-arguments on this topic. The Catholic Church is clear and unchanging in her teaching on this; while on the other side the arguments are the same, at least for the last twenty years.

The articles appeared to me to be the outcome of the struggle for equality, against the male-dominated Church. This struggle is today visible in politics, institutions, families and in every strata of the society. But should we bring down the area of the sacraments too into this realm in order to establish this equality?

The most important argument is the question of the "Persona Christi". The person who represents Christ, the Son of God (not the daughter of God) must be a man, that is the understanding till today. The priest, when he says, "this is my body", repeats the words of Christ. The bread is trans-substantiated into the body of Christ, not because of the goodness of the person who offers the sacrifice or because the person is a man or a woman, but by the power of Christ.

The Church should neither be male-dominated, nor female-dominated but it should be always Spirit-dominated; anything less than this is not spiritual and Christian.

In short, while I am not against ordination of women, I still feel that arguing for it based on inequality, male-domination, better participation in the church, need to have more priests etc., is not fully compatible with the Christian spirit.

George Thomas

Deviated Currents!

Sir,

The Indian Currents started as a Catholic Weekly that was meant mainly for a non-Christian readership. We have other Catholic weeklies for Catholics.

Its purpose was to present the Catholic viewpoint on current issues to the people of influence in politics and the government. Copies were being sent to all the Members of Parliament. It did yeomen service in highlighting the atrocities against Christians and others during the last few years. But of late it has brought out issues that do not put the Church in a good light before the non-Catholics. It came to a head with your articles on women's ordination. To go against what the Holy Father has said is definite Catholic teaching is not expected of your magazine. Perhaps, in a magazine meant for Catholics, articles challenging the official Church teaching may not be as bad.

But for a paper that was originally meant for non-Christians, it serves very little positive purpose. I had asked all the parishes and institutions in the diocese to subscribe to your paper because of its original purpose. But I can't do that if it devotes its issues to attacking the official teaching of the Church.

Bp. Patrick Nair
(Bishop of Meerut)

Congrats to Dr Kottoor

Sir,

Congratulations to Dr Kottoor for his impressive report from Dublin on Women's Ordination Worldwide. Sr. Vladimiroff's statement has certain Benedictine ring to it: "There is a fundamental difference in the understanding of obedience in the monastic tradition and that which is being used by the Vatican to exert power and control and prompt a false sense of unity inspired by fear". When we women become teachers of religious faith, O Lord, how different it sounds!

Dr Kottoor cites two instances of "Vatican's orders" and "pressures". Interesting language in the bosom of the Catholic Church, isn't it? I presume the Roman authorities wanted the nuns to be "nannies in uniforms"! An observation in point: there is an abundance of theological and ascetical literature to indoctrinate lay Christians in the virtue of obedience. But we do not find equally adequate publications and exhortations to the hierarchy with detailed instructions on the proper use of authority. Indeed, an alarming poverty of resources!

If faith should govern men and women in the acceptance of authority and response of obedience, I suppose I would not be a heretic if I say that the same faith ought to equally provide the context necessary for the exercise of authority.

Alphonsa Sebastian, *New York (e-mail)*

Currents flowing straight

Sir,

Bp Patrick Nair censures (IC, 30 July) your weekly for spotlighting "issues that do not put the Church in a good light before the non-Catholics".

As these "issues" are there before the whole world to see, being an ostrich does not help. It is in the normal course of things for human institutions to show forth the fragile nature of the members. The Church is no exception. But what sets the Church apart from its counterparts is not its numerous schools and hospitals but its courage in publicly owning up to its fallenness and in continuously rising up again to carry out its mission of being the light of the world. Which other Christian Church or religion shows the humility to seek the world's pardon for all the ills it has caused even in the distant past? "Many Cardinals and Bishops expressed the desire for a serious examination of conscience above all on the part of the Church of today. On the threshold of the new Millennium Christians need to place themselves humbly before the Lord and examine themselves on the responsibility which they too have for the evils of our day" (John Paul II, Tertio Millennium Adveniente, 36).

Through self-criticism the Church sincerely tries to measure up to the Gospel and build on the Gospel values in the human heart. "The Church serves the Kingdom by spreading throughout the world the 'Gospel values' which are an expression of the Kingdom and which help people to accept God's plan. It is true that the inchoate reality of the Kingdom can also be found beyond the confines of the Church among peoples everywhere, to the extent that they live

'Gospel values' and are open to working of the Spirit who breathes when and where he wills" (John Paul II, Redemptoris Missio, 20). The pope seems to be racing against time in "freeing the Church of the burdens of history" in order to render it a sign of credibility for the world.

In publishing the article "Kottayam Diocese – A Gospel Anomaly" was not the IC pointing the finger at the practice of casteism in the Church, which is incompatible with the Gospel? Has not the Church now given a month's time to Abp Milingo in order to retrace his steps? Was it not a mental block that made the same authorities read "serious errors" in Fr Dupius' book? Hasn't the publication of the articles on women's ordination to priesthood contributed to creating a spirit of discernment in the Church? "But after rumbles of Roman thunder the storm blew by with no reprisals. A week after the conference, the Vatican announced Chittister and Poole would not be punished... it [Vatican] has in effect complied with the conference's first resolution and lifted the ban on discussion" ["Sisters of Defiance", in Time 23 July 2001].

Instead of being scandalised by the Church's humble self-examination, today the world looks up to the Church for ethical leadership precisely because of its humanity and sincerity. Can we now hope that Bishop Patrick Nair will continue asking "all the parishes and institutions in the diocese to subscribe to your paper"?

Asirvadv (on e.mail)

Infallibility of Magisterium

Sir,

In the Indian Currents dated July 22, 2001, among the letters, is one written by Fr. James Pereppadan about the issue of women priests. Having been resident of Western Europe since 1994 he writes from Rome that in Europe it is absolutely a non-issue. In the same issue of IC on Page 20, Dr. James Kottoor writes: "Pope John Paul II had declared in His Encyclical 'Ordination Sacerdotalis' of 1994 that ordination of women as priests·in the Catholic Church was a closed question and that it is to be accepted by all the faithful as the teaching of the infallible ordinary magisterium of the Church".

When the magisterium, of the Catholic Church has spoken why devote so much space to this matter. Do these Catholics have a lurking hope that the Church can be made to taken a U-turn on an infallible teaching? Then what is the meaning of infallibility?

J.C.Kuriacose, Madras

More Catholic than Pope?

Sir,

The Pope in his Encyclical of 1994 clearly says that ordination of women in the Catholic Church as priests is a closed question. Why, then, do you want to bring up this issue? Why try to be more Catholic than the Pope?

Dr.Kottoor says (IC, July 22, 2001) Vatican has not punished the nuns. What a big deal! Vatican has not awarded them with Nobel Prizes either. The Catholic Church is way mightier than a few nuns' senseless prattling. The Church doesn't care disagreements and defiance. She is trying to be perhaps a little more human and understanding by not punishing. The Church is not going to be any better with a few nuns getting ordained.

Stephen Scaria, Bangalore

True Voce of Voiceless!

Sir

Hearty congratulations to you for giving excellent coverage to the International conference convened by WOW at Dublin.

Dr. James Kottoor deserves special credit for the vivid and detailed report. Whereas many Catholic publications have been blind, deaf and dumb to the historical meet, true to your claim as "a voice for the voiceless", you have given a fearless and elaborate "anatomy" of the conference. Truly you are the voice of the voiceless, not only without but also within the church. You cry and shout not only when people are hit by the strident but also when they are beaten with the cross.

Indeed you are to be commended for your concern for justice. Women's ordination in the Catholic Church is not a non-issue, as some would like to have it made out. It is really a core-issue of justice. Like the Benedictine sister Christine Vladimiroff, the Prioress of Sr. Joan Chittister's community, who could not be cowed down by Vatican's intimidations, you have shown the guts to stand for gender equality.

In the Church we must have a sober, Christian view of obedience, which ought to be filial and familial, rather than military and mechanical. In a family, even small children will not obey their parents mechanically. For instance, when a certain stage is reached, children will push aside the feeding hands of their mother and try to eat by themselves, (It is only by learning to eat by themselves they can grow, not by being spoon-fed all the time by their parents.) which is not to be interpreted as owing to their disobedience, pride and ingratitude, but as an indication of their innate urge to grow.

Though a seminarian must obey his rector, it is not to be thought that when the rector plays a game of badminton with him, the seminarian must not try to defeat the rector and must play in such a manner that the rector is always the winner. Let him by all means try to defeat the rector. Then alone the rector will play vigorously and will have good exercise.

When a bishop is suffering on account of rheumatism and has to undergo a course of "Chavittithirummal"(Massaging with feet), the pious Catholic 'Vaidyan' is not to desist from massaging the bishop with his feet, thinking that it will be sacrilegious to do so.Like temples and mosques, churches also have to be swept from time to time. As on the bread of the poor, fungi may appear on the Blessed Sacrament too, if it is not renewed from time to time. The Pope-mobile also must have a reverse gear.

In our body, like the legs, the head also must sweat, and it is not to be thought that the sweat on the head is sweet smelling as different from the sweat on the legs. Even as the legs, the head also needs wash. It is thus with the Mystical Body of Christ too. Popes have erred in the past, as our present Holy Father is humbly acknowledging with his 'mea culpas'.

There was a time when lay people were forbidden to read the Bible, when women were not allowed to be nurses, to take part in athletics, to act in dramas and films. There are some more hurdles on their path to equality. In the 21st century women have come a long way to stand erect on a par with men. Let there be no discrimination in Christian discipleship. We are all one in the Lord. Let those who would like to keep down women remember that it was not from Rome, but at home, not from the Pope with his infallibility, but from their mother, they learnt to pray for the first time, and it was in the love of their parents they had as it were the sacramental experience of the love of the Father/Mother in heaven.

Things have to change. Let there be no more repression and oppression in the name of obedience. Let all gender discrimination end soon. Let us all enjoy the freedom of the children of God and grow to his fullness in love.

Sadhu Ittayavirah, Kerala

Jesus chose no Woman

Sir,

This refers to discussion on Women Priests. The Catholic Church has many intellectual nuns and some nuns have even proved beyond male priests in social service, education, health care, etc.

But ordination of women in the Catholic Church and their cry for the priesthood cannot be and should not be discussed in any

forum. God has made it clear that his ways and thoughts are different from men and women. During the time of Jesus, he did not choose
a single woman among his twelve disciples. However he could have
named any female right from Mary Magdalene / Veronica/ Maratha/
Elizabeth or any women folk close to him. In fact it is they, who
comforted, solaced, soothed the Lord during His passion and tribu-
lation. But yet Jesus did not name any women in his discipleship.
Further it is very explicit on the part of the Saviour to choose men
instead of women for priesthood which is very much evident in revealing Peter that he is a rock and on that rock he will build a church.
Therefore women cannot question the plan of God, which is a mystery. Questioning is tantamount to questioning the divine power. It is
better not to have a discussion, deliberation, contemplation, and
concentration on women priesthood. Therefore dialogue on women
priesthood must be stopped forthwith and follow the precept of
Catholic Church and the spiritual authority of the Pope.

A.C. D'souza, Bangalore

Don't Kill IC Again

Sir,

This has reference to the Letter to the Editor "Deviated Currents" by Bp. Patrick Nair. As a member of the CCI, I was closely
following the growth of IC, in its earlier incarnations, under the
watchful eyes of CBCI, and everyone knows the fate that had
befallen it! And it was gasping for breath for a long time. It would
be more appropriate to say that the Church authorities killed it by
trying to make it a mouthpiece of CBCI.

It was under this trying circumstance that the new management
took over IC. The next few years saw the magazine climbing new
heights both in its content and circulation. Those who are at its
helm of affairs are leaving no stones unturned in upholding human
rights, protecting the rights of minorities, Dalits and the downtrod-
den and above all to remain as the voice of the voiceless. It was in

recognition of its high standards that Indian Currents was conferred the ICPA award recently.

As such, I feel that the CBCI should be happy at the way Indian Currents is growing by leaps and bounds. The Church is accountable to the people around. Any mistakes or malpractice in the Church should be acknowledged publicly. Any publication that comes out is an open document and hence it will not be proper to draw a line of distinction between church view and non-church view and publish the former alone as pointed out by the bishop. The need of the hour is to encourage and promote introspection and healthy criticism. It would be unethical and unprofessional to try to suppress it. Soul searching introspection and aggressive self-criticism is the hallmark of IC and this adds to its credibility before the readers.

If people continue to subscribe to IC, it is not to read the pious exhortation of the bishops. Its readers are not looking forward to the oft-repeated, and often outdated, appeals that emanate from the Church hierarchy. They do look forward to read the news and views that are left uncovered or unnoticed. Quite often such articles and items could go against the established and orthodox views of the powers-that-be. That is the raison d'etre of reading IC.

Hence, my humble request to the honourable Bishop is that he should not make an attempt to kill IC again. Chances are that such attempts would turn out to be abortive. The right approach would be to lend a helping hand in bringing out the magazine week after week. In any case, leave it free to serve its high, noble purpose.

K.L. Mathew, Chennai

Church an empty Tomb?

Sir,

Some readers seem to be thrilled by the campaign of Dr. James Kottoor for women's priesthood. Their supportive feedback must definitely make him happy. But sometimes he is wandering in forbidden lands, I am afraid. In his over-enthusiasm, he talks like a fanatic. He is free to hold and express forcefully his views on any subject. But when it is done within the limits of accepted norms only, it can be appreciated. Ideas must be confronted by ideas, not by mimicry.

In 'Discovering Christ in the Tomb of Church' (IC, 12 August) he alludes, "..... the church which apparently have become a fossil or an empty tomb without His bodily vivifying presence." What does he mean? Is the church dead and forsaken by the Spirit of Christ just because she doesn't fall in line with Kottoor's line of thinking? Again, in the concluding para of the same article, he boasts, "In any case the latest news that the Vatican is not contemplating any punitive action against the sisters seems to prove the adage that a barking dog seldom bites." This kind of expression is childish, if not foolish, least expected of a person of Kottoor's stature and experience. What would he do if, in fact, the sisters concerned were 'bitten'? Kottoor is well aware of the severe and sometimes inhuman punishments imposed on the dissidents and heretics in the past. Expression of dissent and protest should be decent and mature. The actor should not forget the script when the admires applaud.

Mini Kainoor, M.P

Censuring Openness

Sir,

The anger expressed by Bishop Patrick Nair of Meerut on IC for its reporting news and views on the World Conference is symptomatic of the fascist ecclesiastical psyche which reminds us of the days of inquisition. Nowadays it is easy to diagnose such tendencies in India since we have the touchstone of Hindutva fanaticism. Bishop Nair's letter could be easily taken for an RSS leaflet after substituting the names and subjects.

The threatening epistle conveys the advice that the reporting and publishing by IC ought to be positively selective in picking and choosing the topics the official Church would like the readers to read. It means to be negatively selective to the extent to avoid all subjects the official Church may not like the readers to read. According to the Bishop, the subject could be dealt with in house publications for Catholics only. Since the IC is meant for secular readers, the topic ought to have been skirted. We may yet to have the detailed reasoning behind this stand taken by the Bishop.

However, Bishop Nair deserves compliments for his frankness, which is rare among authorities like Bishops whose authority does not depend on any democratic or communitarian processes and accountability. But it was meant to threaten with the penalty of instructing his institutions to unsubscribe. Is this the same Catholic Church, which boasts itself of its docility to the Spirit of truth and advocates dialogue? IC is getting its new Episcopal lesson: Untruth shall make you free. Or to put it differently, if you do not want to lose your subscriptions (need not necessarily the readership, since sisters and priests can read IC by borrowing or hiding it from their Bishop), you better not publish such materials as that of women's priesthood.

Shaji Thomas, Kuwait

Bp. Nair: Genuine Well Wisher

Sir,

It is unfair to allege that Bp Nair's response to some of your articles smacks of fascism (IC, 20-26 August). The bishop's letter, on the other hand, shows that he is a regular reader of the IC, esteems it for its media role, and has been personally promoting it. He has every right to openly regret that, according to him, some of your articles are ill-conceived. His is a voice of a genuine well-wisher and should be listened to.

But the real danger for a Catholic periodical comes from those others who neither read it nor lift a finger to spread it, but are trigger-happy to wield the Episcopal authority against it, if the clique around them so desires. If the editor is a diocesan priest, he may be straightaway given his marching orders; it is the bishop's exclusive prerogative to determine where a priest is to be posted. In this the bishop is not answerable to anyone, not even to the pope. If the editor is a religious, the modus operandi is rather clumsy. The editor's religious superior is summoned and is made to understand the political exigency of transferring him. Fearing for the well being of his Congregation, the superior normally bows to the bishop's wishes. Consequently the editor "goes for higher studies" or "to the Missions". Now it becomes the question of religious obedience and not of editorial policy.

Recently at an intercontinental stopover a globe-trotting Indian bishop reportedly denigrated the IC sweepingly accusing it of being "an irresponsible magazine"; some years back the IC is said to have criticised him for denying official funeral rites to a deceased faithful. It is the likes of him whom you have to be wary of. Instead without compromising on its principled stand, the IC should not alienate those like Bp Nair and intentionally seek to cultivate a rapport with them if it intends to continue effectively functioning as "a voice of the voiceless".

A former editor of a Catholic periodical (Name withheld on request)

Opinion Poll Analysis

Sir,

This is in response to your Opinion Poll result in IC Aug.12th. Being unorthodox I am interested in the subject, especially on behalf of the 80,000 odd Religious Sisters in India who seemingly enjoy a status less than that of the lowly position occupied by the Laity themselves.

At the outset I must congratulate the author, Suresh Pallivathukkal, for his enthusiasm in presenting the poll results. The extremely limited information about the opinion of a miniscule 4400 is interesting and intriguing especially for what it does not tell us. Like a bikini, it promises a lot but reveals hardly anything. May be a temperate language would have vastly improved the quality of this document.

[1]. Was the response really all that overwhelming from across the globe considering that only 4400 responded, and only 46 responded the first day? Experience would have told the author that responses are very much more in the first flush of publicity and then it fades off.

[2] Has the author considered the probability that in such opinion polls some individuals tend to respond again and again to influence the results in the direction they desire? So a 59-41-vote pattern could just be that. As Sir Roger de Coverley would say 'much may be said on both sides'. Have the responses been analyzed for this possibility?

[3] How does a mere two percent or just 88 telephonic contacts add up to reporting that 'our office was flooded with phone calls'?

[5] It is also in extremely bad taste to have dragged in the name of Dr. James Kottoor who is not being 'judged' through a poll. This certainly reflects on the author's immaturity in handling qualitative responses. The subject is ordination of women not Dr. Kottoor.

[6] Again, it is not denied that some respondents are tempted to use the opportunity to comment on irrelevant matters, but responsible writers exclude this extraneous matter to report only the relevant focused comments. If the 'researchers' are so incensed they could write a separate article on what people said about such matters as are relevant to the image of IC.

[7] Status of Participants: This is an example of extremely inadequate and biased reporting. Why has the author withheld some vital identification data and publicized others? What were his cri-

teria for these decisions? For example what is the sex wise distribution of lay and clergy including religious and especially nuns? How are Bishops/Archbishops distributed among the religious/priests? How many Indians and how many foreigners from which countries? How many IC subscribers? How many Non Christians? How many Roman Catholics? Other Christians? Other religious groups? It was not sufficient to give these figures; it is also necessary to report the proportion in each subgroup that voted for or against ordination of women. The argument 'promised to keep the identity of the respondents confidential, we are unable to give more details of the participants,' is a very weak argument. Why were identification data collected in the first place? Is there a hidden purpose in collecting this information? If 'opaqueness' is evident, then the researcher's purpose is suspect. If there is no intention to use the identifying data to analyze and report the results then, like the daily news papers, the author should have just reported so many for and so many against. In any case if confidentiality is being preserved why any information about Indian-foreign differential voting, male female differential voting etc? But to say that one will not reveal the sex-wise lay and clergy differences leaves much to be desired.

One result is clear: 59 percent disfavour, 41 percent support ordination. And readers are told that 'there were interesting variations in the way various categories of people responded to the issue'.

[8] Method of Response: Here again, the author has focused on this important aspect of the study and therefore he should have taken a further step. For example, he could have addressed such questions as: whether there are differences in voting depending on the mode used for voting.Incidentally, 4000 odd just represent themselves and not 'people of God'. It is such sweeping comments that distract from the quality of the article.

[9] Extracts of the Comments: The author has selected and re-

ported some comments. How many made comments? Of these how many were in favour and how many were conditional and how many against? In other words which subgroup was more articulate?

P. Ramachandran, Bombay

(**Editor's Note:** We appreciate the interest taken by Prof. P.Ramachandran in the Women's Ordination Opinion Poll Result, and the valuable suggestions given in his letter. We are taking these suggestions with great seriousness and will keep them in mind for any such later project.

However, the simple answer to his many queries is that this Poll was not meant to be a strict scientific survey. Its primary objective was to assess the general reaction of the readers. That is why the data asked for in the questionnaire were very general and so the answers too were of that tenor. And so we believe that the purpose of the Poll has been, by and large, achieved satisfactorily.)

Web sites on Women Priests

Sir:

Regardless of what Bishop Patrick Nair feels is inappropriate for IC to discuss, the truth of the matter is that the ordination of women in the Catholic Church is an issue that is being examined and debated on several other [Indian] fora.

At about the same time IC was reporting on the Women priests debate, a debate was taking place on the AASRAINDIA@yahoo groups.com discussion group and it was a lively participation by both men and women heavily slanted in favour of having women priests, though there were a lot of interesting points raised both ways.

We'd like to remind the good Bishop that for all the Bishops and Popes of the Roman Catholic Church did in centuries past to censor even scientific data to suit their interpretation of the universe, the fact is, in the muttered words of Galileo, "The earth still revolves around the sun, whether I acknowledge it or not." The politics within and without the curia and the archdiocese is a topic of discussion and debate among Catholics and others, whether the good Bishop acknowledges it or not. And by the way, in the church I visit, we still say, "Our Father in heaven, holy be your name..." because we, the people feel that is more relevant.

Frank Krishner, Patna

Women at Last Supper

Sir,

The traditional pictures of the Last Supper we all are used to seem to have missed out something. That dawned on me only when I looked at the beautiful pictures of the Last Supper you published in IC in connection with WOW.They struck me as unforgettable, because I saw in them "something" which I never saw in other pictures — yes also women in that group duly serving the Lord, waiting on Him and participating at the table with the Bread and Wine. That woke me up to realise that I was not missing "something" but "some people" in earlier pictures.

It seems a great thing to think that women were not kept out of the Last Supper by the Lord. Otherwise, women could very well be left out of even receiving the Eucharist now and some one could justify it saying that Christ never did it. Mother Teresa's biographers record that the Mass and Eucharist was the food that sustained her through all her difficulties, even to the end of her life.

Santa, Ernakulam

Masterly Journalism

Sir,

I was following Dr. Kottoor's detailed reporting and write-ups on crucial current issues in the "Indian Currents" including the latest on the Tehelka discoveries.

"Frankly Speaking" is always interesting since his hard punches are delivered smilingly. The writings on women's ordination are much appreciated. So too is what he wrote on the comments of Bishop Patrick Nair and his edict. Thank goodness for his masterly journalism!

Carmel, U.P.

* * *

20

Critical Loyalty and Loyal Criticism,not blind 'Yes'

Critics Help Strengthen Weak Defenses!

Dr. James Kottoor

What is the strength of a chain? It is its weakest link, which would be the first to give way. We all have our strong points or fronts. So too we have our weak, weaker and weakest points. Unless we identify and fortify these points starting with the weakest we are bound to cave in when pressure is mounted on our weakest front – physical, intellectual or moral. What is true of individuals is also true of institutions, organizations, parties, states and nations.

Conversely our strength consists in discovering our weaknesses through self-examination, self-criticism or criticism from well-meaning or even ill-meaning people. A critic deserves to be respected, esteemed, encouraged and thanked profusely because more often than not his services are offered free, not paid for, and therefore considered thankless. In the absence of such free wheeling critics, we all would have to invent or engage the services of a devil's advocate, if we are sincerely concerned and keen about improving ourselves and becoming perfect on all fronts.

Like a storm in a teacup we have been witnessing waves and waves of criticism in our letter to Editor Columns. It augurs well for the critics, for the criticized and for the Indian Currents (IC). At least it means IC is being read and what is read provokes people to think and ask questions which are the preliminary steps in the process of healthy, constructive thinking and learning. That we have to learn from everyone else till our last breath, no body can deny. Weather all are willing to do it is a different question. Even in our field of specialization our knowledge is ever so incomplete. Hence the saying: the biggest room in this world is the room for improvement which none of us shall ever succeed to fill.

Thanks to Questioners

The recently held Dublin conference on Women's Ordination Worldwide, the first of its kind in the Roman Catholic Church seems to have stirred up a hornet's nest for many well-meaning persons. Some of them had the courage of their convictions to come out and defend their views for or against openly. All of them deserve to be admired, commended and thanked. Bishop Patrick Nair of Meerut deserves special mention. He had the grace and courage to go public with his convictions while his peers did not. Although he was airing his personal views, surely those views are subscribed to with minor alterations by many other bishops. Only they did not articulate them for various reasons. Even they benefited from his expressed views, just as all the apostles benefited from the questions of a doubting Thomas. That the church should not be presented in bad light especially before non-Christians, that we should present a façade of unity even in matters where the so-called believers are totally divided, are views held by many bishops, priests and people. Others may think that what is important is not good or bad light but true light since Christ came to bear witness to unalloyed truth which is often a bitter pill, a two edged sword. There never was, is and will never be an ideal church as long as it is going to be made up of frail human beings. The more it is prepared to confess and say "mea Culpa" and get up from its failures as eminently demonstrated by the present Holy Father, the more it is bound to perfect itself and attract the attention and admiration not only of the nominal Christians but also of the entire humanity.

Similarly views such as: Dad Knows best, believe the H.Father, don't use the scalpel of reason, Women's Ordination is a non-issue and it should not be discussed, the Church is unchangeable, can there be a U-turn on what is said to be an infallible teaching, questioning the teachings of the church is questioning God – are not just stray views of a few individuals who demonstrated their courage to go public with their honest beliefs and convictions. Many others also share these views. There is no harm in re-examining these deeply cherished beliefs under the piercing, dissecting light of reason which God has given to each for use and not to bury in the ground. Questioning is not denying. It is the first step in every scientific enquiry and discovery in the development of doctrine. What harm if one tries to prove that God does not exist, in order to strengthen or discredit the belief of some in a living God? Only he should not come to blows propelled by fanaticism or infallibility complex. What is important is to reach a consensus by learning to agree or disagree in an agreeable way and reduce the area of conflict. For this all should be prepared to go through the long, tedious and uncertain process of discussion for the sake of new discoveries.

Loyalty and Criticism

Loyalty and criticism are not two mutually eliminating concepts even as charity and truth are not. What befits rational human nature is loyal criticism and critical loyalty, pursuit of the whole truth in all charity, not throwing away the baby with the bathwater, not blind faith but an enlightened understanding in spite of the Ignatian prescription: "What seems to me white, I will believe black if the hierarchal church so defines" which can be nothing but an insult to intelligence because, "a custom without truth is nothing but an ancient error,"(Cyprian). What is important is "unity in necessary things, diversity in unnecessary things and charity in all things"(St.Augustine), and this unity in essentials is within the reach of man because truth and mind are meant for and made for each other, and when honest discussions are not only permitted but encouraged truth is bound to be exposed flawlessly before the human mind and once they are made to confront each other eye-ball to eye-ball they will be automatically and powerfully drawn into each other like the north and south poles of magnets. Hence the saying: Truth is a trap, to go too near it, to see it unalloyed is to be trapped by it, to be sucked into it leading to something akin to a falling in love at first sight, consent, consummation and bliss.

It is also one of the cardinal teachings of the Church that one should, in the final analysis, follow his commanding conscience in choosing between right and wrong. One may study, meditate, pray and consult the whole world but must seek God, goodness and truth propelled by his own commanding mind, not by the mind of his superior, inferior, friend or foe. It is in doing this that the Prioress Vladimiroff and the Benedictine community has set a magnificent example. And Vatican's decision not to impose any punishment should be seen as a recognition of this principle of concern for both truth and charity, loyal criticism and critical loyalty.

What about the apparent conflict and confrontation between the Vatican and the religious congregations of Sr. Joan and Sr.Myra on the 'infallibility' issue connected with the current church teaching on Women's ordination? The danger here is in equating the Vatican with the Pope, Pope with Christ, Christ with the Church and church with the people of God – all true partially - and projecting the present conflict as one between the Pope and his faithful or Christ and his believers. Watchdogs are common in many homes. Sometimes they not only bark at but also bite, not only intruders but also even friends of the householder. In all such cases the householder is blamed although he may have never barked at anyone. Similarly it is wrong to blame the Pope for all the barks and bites taking place between the Vatican officials and various sections of the church. That is why Pope John XXIII once said: "I am only the Pope." And the present Pope is bound to go down in

History as the Confessing Pope, the Pope of "mea culpas" which were none of his failures but of the various structures, including the offices of the Vatican and of the Institutional church.

Past Precedents

If something has been done in the past it can be done again. *(Ab esse ad posse valet illatio.)* Care should be taken not to repeat the mistakes of the past while efforts should be made to promote good precedents. The advocates of women's ordination point out with historical evidence that women were ordained deacons and priests in the past. Recently a book narrating the story of a Roman Catholic woman ordained priest for the underground church in the communist Czechoslovakia has also come out. If these are facts beyond dispute how can anyone say now that the Church has no authority to ordain women? This is one of the cruxes of the many arguments brought up by the advocates of women's ordination.

If the Holy Spirit is guiding the church there should be consensus and not conflict at various levels of the Church on the present infallibility issue. But consensus is something to be arrived at through discussion to clarify conflicting perceptions. This has not taken place at the Episcopal or hierarchical level although a lot of it is going on at the level of theologians and scripture scholars. It is the freedom of the children of God that makes it both a right and a duty to engage in discussion and dialogue until clarity emerges and the people of God led by the women folk of today seems to have taken the lead to get the hierarchy moving to get a closer look even at the infallibility of Infallibility. A better understanding of it can never be wrong as long as everyone believes in the role of the sensus fidelium in the development of doctrine.

There remain a section of spirited and concerned contributors to the letter to editor columns who deserve to be specially lauded for joining in to throw light on various perplexing questions with enlightening examples and explanations. More strength to their pen.

What about those who wait on the sidelines to watch and the mute spectators of this drama? They also contribute their lion's share because those who stand and wait or watch also serve. What is a drama without these spectators called the People of God? What is a battalion with Generals only!

* * *

21

Tea Shop Chats!

Women Priests

Anoop Dev

("Tea-shop Chats" is a dramatic presentation of the socio-political, religio-cultural situation of the country. The words uttered by the characters do not necessarily reflect the actual sayings of the real persons, though the tend is hinted at. This may be classified as socio-religious satire. Here there is no intention of hurting any individual or group.)

Journalist: The Pope is a spiritual guerilla, or I would say, a spiritual autocrat, it seems.

Politician: How can he keep together his vast spiritual and material empire without strong measures, strong will and a clear vision?

Theologian: Don't expect clear vision from an octogenarian.

Politician: What I meant was his mental vision, his ideological alertness.

Theologian: But he is adamantly adhering to his pet visions. He doesn't lead the church according to the signs of the time.

Layman: What are the signs of the time you are pointing to?

Theologian: Freedom of conscience, equality of sex, new scientific awareness of man and his changed ethical value system etc.

Layman: The Pope is the greatest advocate of the freedom and dignity of man.

Scholar: That is peripheral. Radical change is the need of the time.

Rabbi: He's the greatest Pope in modern times. He was generous enough to ask pardon for the sins of commissions and omissions committed against our people in the past.

Mulla: I was much edified to see him praying in a Mosque

Politician: His mass appeal is tremendous.

Layman: He is sincere and forthright.

Theologian: But he is the prisoner of dogmas, prisoner of his own ideas.

Layman: But his ideas are based on scripture and tradition, and he is duty-bound to uphold the dogmas of the church.

Scholar: What do you know about the background of how dogmas were developed and defined? You lay people are satisfied with some popular devotions based on some imaginary stories called visions.

Layman: Don't ridicule our simple faith. The apostles were not scholars and theologians.

Theologian: That is not a credit either. The dull-headedness of the apostles has negatively affected the progressive thinking of the Church.

Scholar: Over the centuries what one comes across is suppression of freedom and repression of intellectual pursuit, be it in philosophy, theology or science. Reason was made servant of faith. And faith remained obscure.

Layman: How can you deny the existence of great thinkers and their great works in the past? Of course restrictions were there. But that was to safeguard the content of faith from getting dissipated. The official church has had great responsibility to keep the faith entrusted to it.

Scholar: Faith is not the monopoly of the Pope. Church is not confined to the Vatican curia. Every believer is an active part of the Church. Faith-content is entrusted to the Church, not to the Pope alone.

Layman: But it should not lead to individualism. If the Church is a community of believers, a leader should guide that community. That is the role of the Pope.

Politician: I don't know much about the past. The present Pope is a widely respected person. Even his critics respect him.

Rabbi: He was instrumental to the crumbling down of the once great Soviet Union.

Politician: I remember once Stalin asked how many divisions the Pope had got. He was ridiculing the ruler of the Vatican City. But see the irony. A Pope with no military division behind him pulls down the mighty communist block!

Theologian: These are all pleasantries and platitudes. The Church is facing serious problems.

Journalist: Could you elaborate?

Theologian: Take for example, the question of women priests, homosexuals, use of condom, birth control, and human cloning. The Pope has to take a well-informed and definite stand on these vital issues.

Mulla: I think the Pope has expressed his views on these subjects clearly and unequivocally. We appreciate his stand.

Politician: His stand may be debated. Yet in a world of fluid morality, the voice of the Pope stands like a solid rock. Even his staunch critics appreciate his lucidity and firmness in matters of morals.

Mulla: That's why he was declared the Man of the Year some time back.

Rabbi: He's the Man of the Millennium.

Theologian: But his firmness is not supported by sound theological research. Rigidity is the enemy of freedom and growth.

Journalist: Where is this rigidity reflected most?

Theologian: See for example, the official position of the Church on women priests and homosexuals is too rigid and against the current theological thinking.

Scholar: Let's discuss the question of women priests first.

Politician: 'Women priests' is an interesting subject. Even in our field women are fighting for special quota. They are now in a fighting mood. They want to overthrow the centuries old male dominance and assert their equality in every field.

Rabbi: There are some basic inequalities in nature. You cannot change them.

Journalist: What is that?

Rabbi: Males cannot bear children and breast-feed them. There are biological and psychological differences between male and female. What is needed is understanding and cooperation. The basic concept of the Bible about man and woman is beautiful.

Politician: What's that?

Rabbi: According to the creation story, God formed man out of soil; but he formed woman not out of another heap of soil, but out of man. And man acknowledges: "This is now bone of my bones and flesh of my flesh." So intimately they are related. There is no superiority or subordination. Together they have to develop and govern the universe.

Scholar: But man was made first and woman as a secondary being out of a single rib. God could have created woman also from the same soil to show the equality of the sexes.

Rabbi: Our problem is sometimes we go for literal interpretation of the Bible and miss the essential message. And if God formed woman out of man, it was his plan and he is giving us a powerful message. Who are we to question him? We are clay and he is the potter.

Theologian: Coming to the present issue, we can come across women priests in all religions.

Layman: What about the Orthodox Churches?

Rabbi: We don't have women priests.

Mulla: We too don't have.

Scholar: Semitic religions are biased against women.

Politician: What are your arguments for ordaining women as priests?

Theologian: There is no man-woman difference in Jesus. Theologically speaking, just like man, woman also can act in the person of Christ. The quality signified by the priest is not Christ's maleness, but his role as mediator. This can and should be signified also by women priests. Women are equal in Christ; women too bear Christ's image; women already act as another Christ as ministers of baptism and marriage; women reflect better Christ's feminine traits; women too can represent Christ's love which is the essence of his priesthood.

Scholar: There is a latent and dynamic tradition in the church implying the possibility of women's ordination to priesthood. This is reflected in the practice of ordaining some women as deaconesses in the early centuries; in Mary's perceived priestly functions; in the devotion to Mary Magdalene who was seen as a woman minister; through women administering baptism and matrimony; in the unbroken awareness of the equality of men and women in Christ.

Journalist: Then how is that priesthood is not yet conferred upon women?

Theologian: Rome denies priesthood to women saying that Jesus Christ did not call any woman to be part of the twelve apostles. It is a permanent norm of priesthood established by Christ and so Church has no authority to ordain women, Rome asserts.

Scholar: There are arguments from Scripture, Tradition, Theology and Magisterium on the side of Rome. But Rome's assessment of the Church's authority regarding the ordination of women priests is mistaken.

Politician: But the Pope is infallible, it is heard.

Theologian: In very special and limited circumstances, the Pope has the gift of infallibility. It means that, when he is speaking as the supreme teacher of the Church, he can be, provided that all the required conditions apply, the official spokesman of the community of believers, whose common faith is the basic carrier of infallibility.

Scholar: Roman authorities, including Popes, have made serious misjudgments in the past.

Politician: For example?

Theologian: The Church defended slavery as willed by God; she claimed that no one could be saved outside communion with the Catholic Church; she taught that it was wrong to take interest for money lent to other people. The blanket condemnation of homosexuality as evil is another error. There are also terrible mistakes of judgment and crimes of injustice perpetrated with the sanction of the Popes like the inquisition, the persecution of witches and the treatment of priests applying for marriage.

Scholar: The present Roman authorities move on the same line. They have not understood the precious new values of our own time or the need of a more democratic way of governing the Church.

Journalist: What is your comment on this issue?

Layman: On both sides there are arguments and counter arguments. Single line statements do not give justice to the issues under discussion. Our present subject is women's ordination. I look to the Bible. The Catholic Church denies priesthood to women, primarily because Jesus did not call any woman to be part of the apostolic group.

Journalist: What was the reason?

Theologian: The reason why Jesus did not choose women to be part of the twelve apostles was his need to adapt, in this matter, to the social perceptions of the time. For Jesus' contemporaries were under the influence of the social and cultural spell of male predominance.

Politician: But he was a social revolutionary, it is said?

Layman: He was not a revolutionary. But he wanted to revolutionize the thinking of the society.

Theologian: Yet he allowed and accepted many of the existing social evils, disparities and superstitions.

Journalist: For example?

Theologian: He didn't say a word against the Roman colonialism. He didn't do away with slavery. He based most of his teaching on the existing Jewish beliefs many of which had no scientific standing.

Layman: But the thrust of Jesus' teaching wasn't to establish a scientifically enlightened world or to proclaim political freedom. He didn't promise material prosperity and worldly happiness to his followers. His prime concern was the introduction of the Kingdom of God. He based it on justice, truth and love. And it transcended all socio-political considerations.

Scholar: But how will the kingdom of God flourish when its members are immersed in superstitions, social evils and ignorance?

Layman: To my mind, Jesus had given sufficient warnings against social evils and clear guidelines for authentic human life. Of course, except in one case, he didn't use force.

* * *

22

Epilogue

Dr. James Kottoor

What could be the shape of things to come for the advocates of Women's Ordination (WO) in the foreseeable future? As long as the supporters and the opponents of WO are locked in an irreconcilable controversy both can't claim to be guided by the Spirit because the Spirit that guides or ought to guide the church is not one of conflict but of consensus and reconciliation. This stage can be reached only if both sides are prepared to accept defeat for their present positions and let truth to come out victorious.

Truth is mighty and will prevail. It should be made to prevail. It can be made to prevail as long as honest and open discussions are allowed to continue at various levels and not by suppressing debate. Only, those engaged in these discussions should be led by the motto: A friend of truth first and friend of Plato second and disown any monopoly to the whole truth. As things are, some think, that the advocates of WO are on a winning spree. But how realistic are their hopes and expectations? Let us push their arguments to their logical conclusions.

Chasing a Mirage?

If and when women are admitted to the totality of ministerial priesthood, there is bound to be a flood of women priests. The next step would be women bishops which eventually should lead them to the pinnacle of the hierarchical structure in the Catholic Church, a Woman Pope, pregnant or otherwise.

Then suppose they suddenly come to discover that after all they were actually chasing a mirage in the desert and nothing more, because Christ never instituted a hierarchical, pyramidal priesthood, (some theological and scriptural schools of thought have already come to that conclusion and it is stressed even in the letter of the 14 Indian Sisters to the Pope. cf. chapter 6); that He actually came to destroy the hierarchical Judaic Priesthood of His times together with their concepts of sacred places, sacred persons, sacred things and sacred times; that He never called himself a priest or called his pick of 12 or 72 with that title but disciples and followers; that at the last supper He was not instituting a new pyramidal priesthood at all but actually turning the then existing pyramidal Jewish religious structure upside down, making it an inverted pyramid when He the Lord and Master, the one who should have been at the pinnacle of power and hierarchical top position, knelt down before Peter the Rock and broke it to smithereens, not with an iron fist or hammer but with the power of His persuasion, the power of His personality, the power of His graceful descent to all possible and imaginable depths to wash his feet; that true liturgical worship of God the Father is to be done in spirit and in truth in the cave of one's heart with closed doors and not on this mountain or that, not in this temple or that basilica with open doors for public exhibition; that the only church worth speaking of is the Domestic Church run by Domestic Priests called Man and Woman, Husband and Wife, Father and Mother making the bread by the sweat of their brow and breaking the bread to feed the hungry at home and around; that the only pure unspoilt religion in God's sight is to help orphans and widows in need(Jas.1.27); that it was for this reason that Christ preferred to present himself not as the founder of a religion but as the Son of Man(85 times as opposed to Son of God only 38 times), the Ideal Man, the Man for all seasons, climes, countries and peoples of the world and not just for a particular chosen people called Jews, Christians, Catholics or Churches. Is it therefore possible that today's vociferous advocates of WO might not meet with such a disappointing find at the end of their wild-goose chase tomorrow or some twenty years from now?

Humane Secularism

What is important anyway? Priesthood with its pretentious titles or servant-hood fleeing the glare of all publicity and limelight? Not only the traditional understanding of priesthood but also concepts like sacraments, church, and even religion itself are undergoing a sea-change. Old concepts are crumbling and new ones are emerging. Religion itself is losing its sacred halo today among the thinking sections because of the fanaticism and divisive role it plays to set followers of one religion against those of another instead of its becoming the dynamic glue to hold together peoples and nations with a vice-like grip. The biggest casualty of this conflict and violence unleashed in many of the world's danger spots has been the snapping of the tenuous hold these once noble concepts like religion, priestly class and God-men used to have on the minds of people and the tightening of grips in its stead by the votaries of secularism, materialism, agnosticism and even atheism.

While the fanatics of various religions are putting up a brave front and exerting herculean efforts to salvage their sinking ship, the forces of a humane secularism is busy launching a new spacious Titanic with enough elbow room into which all peoples – black and white, rich and poor, educated and illiterate, believers and unbelievers, theists and atheists – of this world can rush in to enthrone, worship and serve their new God called the Dignity and Brotherhood of Man to continue their onward journey peacefully in this new era of globalisation. Their one professed objective is to save, not merely the souls of individual sinners, races, groups or communities but the hopes and aspirations of all nations from being reduced to the hell of global warming in the literal and figurative sense, through the sins of omission and commission, especially by the Diveses of this globe, exploiting the world's meager resources for selfish ends at the expense of the less privileged Lazaruses. The redeeming element in this conflict is the unostentatious religiosity or the sober but true religious zeal which continues to animate and shine forth in the votaries of secularism as opposed to the forces of secularisation, materialism and atheism all of which with their total unconcern for any spiritual values have succeeded only in the break up peoples and nations like the former soviet block. Secularism instead, which accords equal respect and treatment to all true religions and legitimate socio-cultural aspirations and convictions – which can only be complimentary and not conflicting — is bound to make its triumphal march while materialism and other related isms which disown the power of the spiritual, the other-worldly and the eternal in human affairs are bound to come to grief. For it is the spiritual which makes the human humane.

Religious Pluralism

Besides today we don't any more fight bitterly saying there is no salvation outside the church thanks to a new understanding of what ought to constitute the true ingredients of salvation if it is to makes sense to all. While some speak of Exclusivism (Christ the sole Redeemer) others speak of Inclusivism(Anonymous Christianity, which embraces honest believers of all religions) and a third group speaks of Pluralism(those guided solely by conscience and conviction) and sees salvation within the easy reach of all, even unbelievers and atheists, who live according to what they honestly perceive as Truth. For Christians who believe in God's universal will of salvation, Christ's mission to redeem the whole world and affirm that His grace reaches out to all through his commandments of do's and don'ts written in tablets of flesh in the hearts and minds in every man, in case anyone happens to be unaware of the light of revelation, even pluralism should pose no problem. After all didn't even Christ say that he was the Truth, that he came to bear witness to Truth, that those who are not against him(Truth) are with him, that he came as the Son of Man meaning that his mission was to present to the world a perfect example (I have given you an example) of the ideal human life, a truly humane humanity? Nothing more, nothing less!

If a divided Christianity, the multiplicity of churches and fanatical followers of various religions fighting among themselves have become an eye-sore to many it is because they have all strayed away from the truth. Therefore one may wonder how many of the present concepts like priesthood, sacraments, church and religion which are falling into disrepute, are going to make sense to thinking sections of people living two or three decades from now in an age of post-ecumenical Christianity or post religious humane humanity. "Because the church of Jesus Christ may not be called to ordained priesthood as we know it now, but the church of Christ is always, undoubtedly, surely called to true discipleship," according to Sr.Joan Chittister. When priesthood itself as we know it today is questioned what is the relevance of fighting for the ordination of women? Is it not like rushing into a sinking ship? In short an infallible Pope confessing the sins and failures of his infallible church may well be the trend setter for the shape of things to come because is not change alone and growth through change the unchangeable law of nature? "In a higher world it is otherwise, but here below to live is to change, and to be perfect is to have changed often!"(Cardinal Newman)

* * *

Part IV

Appendix

23

Discipleship for a Priestly People in a Priestless Period!

Sr. Joan Chittister, osb

Three stories may explain these reflections on discipleship in an interim age best: The first is about a sweet old woman who had a unique - but somewhat dangerous - habit of making right hand turns from left hand lanes. They say the last time the guy in the cadillac she smashed into broadside, got out of his car, walked around the front, leaned over the driver's window and said, "Lady, just tell me, why didn't you signal?" And the old lady looked up at him and said, "Because, sonny, I always turn here."

The second story is from the Zen poet Basho who wrote: "I do not seek to follow in the footsteps of those of old; I seek the things they sought."

And the third is from ancient monastic literature: Once upon a time, the story goes, a minister traveled with great difficulty to a far away monastery because there was an old monastic there who had a reputation for asking very piercing spiritual questions. "Holy one," the minister said. "Give me a question that will renew my soul." "Ah, yes, then," the old monastic said, "your question is 'what do they need?'" The minister wrestled with the question for days but then, depressed, gave up and went back to the old monastic in disgust. "Holy one," the minister said, "I came here because I'm tired and depressed and dry. I didn't come here to talk about my

ministry. I came here to talk about my spiritual life. Please give me
another question." "Ah, well, of course. Now I see," the old monastic said, "In that case, the right question for you is not 'what do
they need?' The right question for you is 'What do they really need?'"

That question haunts me. What do the people really need in a
period when the sacraments are being lost in a sacramental church
but all approaches to the question—even the admission that there
is an admissible question about the nature and meaning of priesthood is being blocked, obstructed, denied, and suppressed?

"What do they really need?" becomes a haunting refrain in me
for more reasons than the philosophical. Up at the top of a Mexi-
can mountain, up beyond miles of rutted road and wet, flowing
clay, I toured an Indian village that was visited by a priest only
once a year. But that was years ago. Now the mountain is just as
high but the priest is fifteen years older.

Five years ago I spoke in an American parish of 6000 families—one of those new western phenomenon known as 'mega-
churches' that is served by three priests. There is no priest shortage there however, the priests want you to know, because the
bishop has redefined the optimum ratio of priest to people from
one to every 250 families to one priest to every 2000 families.

In diocese after diocese parishes are being merged, closed,
turned into sacramental way stations, being served by retired priests
or married male deacons, both of which are designed to keep the
church male, whether it is ministering or not. The number of priests
is declining: the number of Catholics is increasing; the number of
lay ministers being certified is rising in every academic system despite the fact that their services are being restricted, rejected or
made redundant in parish after parish than ever before.

And here in Pennsylvania there's a five year old girl who, when
her parents answered her question about the absence of women
priests in their parish with the flat explanation that "We don't have

girl-priests in our church, darling," the little girl thought for a minute and then responded quite simply but sharply, "Then why do we go there?!"

Clearly, the church is changing even while it reasserts its change-lessness. But static resistance is a far cry from the dynamism of the early church in which Prisca, and Lydia, and Thecla, and Phoebe and hundreds of women like them, opened house churches, walked as disciples of Paul, "constrained him," the scripture says, to serve a given region, instructed people in the faith and ministered to the fledgling Christian communities with no apology, no argument, no tricky theological shell games about whether they were ministering 'in persona Christi' or 'in nomine Christi'.

Clearly, both the question and the answer are clear: What do they really need? They need what they needed when the temple became more important than the Torah. They need what they needed when the faith was more a vision than an institution. They need what they have always needed: they need community, not patriarchal clericalism; they need the sacred, not the sexist; they need the human, not the homophobic. The people need more prophets of equality, not more pretenders to a priesthood of male privilege. They need discipleship, not canonical decrees.

So what is to be done at a time like this when what is being sought and what is possible are two different things? To what are we to give our energy when we are told no energy is wanted? The questions may sound new but the answer is an old one, an ancient one, a true one. The answer is discipleship. The fact is that we cannot possibly have a "renewed priesthood" unless we have a renewed discipleship in ourselves and around us - around us and in us as well. The temptation is to become weary in the apparently fruitless search for office. But the call is to become recommitted to the essential, the ancient, the authentic demands of discipleship. To renew priesthood, we must revive discipleship. If we seek the ordination that Jesus gives, we must pursue three things:

1.   we must understand the nature of discipleship;

2.   we must recognize the signs of true discipleship and

3.   we must be willing to give ourselves over to what discipleship demands now.

What is discipleship? Christian discipleship is by nature a very
dangerous thing. It has put every person who ever accepted it at
risk. It made every follower who ever took it seriously on alert for
rejection, from Martin of Tours to John Henry Newman, from
Mary Ward to Dorothy Day. Discipleship casts every fragile new
Christian community in tension with the times in which it grows. In
the early church to be a Christian community meant to defy Roman imperialism, to stretch Judaism itself, to counter pagan values
with Christian ones. It demanded very concrete presence; it took
great courage, unending fortitude and clear public posture. Real
discipleship meant the rejection of real things: it meant the rejection of emperor worship, the foreswearing of animal sacrifice, the
inclusion of Gentiles, the elimination of dietary laws, the disavowal
of circumcision, the acceptance of women and the supplanting of
law with love, of nationalism with universalism, of a chosen people
with a global people - YOU! Then, the following of Christ was not
an excursion into the intellectual, it was real and immediate and
cosmic. It was not easy then and it will not be easy now.

The problem with Christian discipleship is that instead of simply requiring a kind of academic or ascetic exercise - the implication of most other kinds of 'discipleship' - Christian discipleship
requires a kind of living that is sure, eventually, to tumble a person
from the banquet tables of prestigious boards and the reviewing
stands of presidents, and the processions of ecclesiastical knighthood to the most suspect margins of both church and society. To
follow Jesus, in other words, is to follow the one who turns the
world upside down, even the religious world. Real discipleship is
a tipsy arrangement at the very least. People with high need for
approval, social status, and public respectability need not apply.

Following Jesus is a circuitous route that leads always and everywhere to places where a 'nice' person would not go, to moments of integrity we would so much rather do without. The disciple carries a worldview that cries for fulfillment now. Christian discipleship is not preparation for the hereafter or an ecstatic distance from the present. Christian discipleship is the commitment to live a gospel life, a marginal life in this place, at this time whatever the cost. To follow Christ is to set about fashioning a world where the standards into which we have been formed become, too often, the very standards we must ultimately foreswear. Flag and fatherland, profit and power, chauvinism and sexism, clericalism and authoritarianism done in the name of Christ are not Christian virtues whatever the system that looks to them for legitimacy.

Christian discipleship is about living in this world the way that Jesus the Christ lived in his - touching lepers, raising donkeys from ditches on Sabbath days, questioning the unquestionable and - consorting with women! Discipleship implies a commitment to leave nets and homes, positions and securities, lordship and legalities to be now - in our own world - what the Christ was for his. The true disciple hears the poor, and ministers to anyone, to everyone, in this world who having been used up by the establishment are then abandoned to make their way alone, unnoticed in a patriarchal world, unwanted in a patriarchal world but mightily, mightily used by a patriarchal world that abuses power, to garner profits both immoral and unconscionable. Discipleship is prepared to fly in the face of a world bent only on maintaining its own ends whatever the cost. If discipleship is what you're here for, be not fooled! The price is a high one and history has recorded it faithfully. Teresa of Avila, John of the Cross and Joan of Arc were persecuted for opposing the hierarchy itself - and then later canonized by them. Discipleship cost Mary Ward her health, her reputation and even a Catholic burial. Discipleship cost Martin Luther King, Jr. his life. No doubt about it, the nature of discipleship is passion and risk.

But to understand the nature of discipleship is not enough. We must be marked by its mark. And what is the mark of true discipleship? True discipleship says the truth in hard times. To the true disciple the problem is clear: The church must not only preach the gospel, it must not obstruct it. It must be what it says. It must demonstrate what it teaches. It must be judged by its own standards. The church that silently colludes with the dispossession of the poor or the economic enslavement of the foreign or racial other in the name of patriotism or citizenship becomes just one more instrument of the state. The church that blesses oppressive governments in the name of obedience to an authority that denies the authority of conscience makes itself an oppressor as well. The church that goes mute in the face of massive militarization practiced in the name of national defense abandons the commitment to the God of love for the preservation of the civil religion. The church that preaches the equality of women but does nothing to demonstrate it within its own structures, that proclaims a theology of equality but insists on an ecclesiology of superiority is out of sync with its best self and dangerously close to repeating the theological errors that underlay centuries of church sanctioned slavery.

The pauperization of women in the name of the sanctity and the essentialism of motherhood flies in the face of the Jesus who overturned tables in the temple, contended with Pilate in the palace, chastised Peter to put away his sword and, despite the teaching of that day, cured the woman with the issue of blood and refused to allow his own apostles to silence the Samaritan women on whose account, Scripture tells us, "Thousands believed that day." Indeed, the life of Jesus shows us, the invisibility of women in the church threatens the very nature of the church itself.

Obviously, discipleship is not based on sexism. It's not based on cultural norms. It's not based on private piety. On the contrary. Discipleship pits the holy against the mundane. It pits the heart of Christ against the heartlessness of an eminently male-oriented, male-defined and male-controlled, world. And that is not the model Scripture gives us of true discipleship. To be a disciple in the model of Judith and Esther, of Deborah and Ruth, of Måry and Mary Magdalene means to find ourselves makers of a world where the weak confound the strong. The true disciple begins like the prophet Ruth to shape a world where the rich and the poor share the garden according to their needs. The true disciple sets out like the judge Deborah to forge a world where the last are made first and the first are last - starting with themselves.

The true disciple insists, as the commander Judith did, on a world where women do what heretofore has been acceptable only for men simply because men said so! To the disciple who follows in the shadow of Esther, as much the savior of her people as Moses was of his, the reign of God - the welcome of the outcast, the reverence of the other, the respect for creation - becomes a foreign land made home. "Come, follow me" becomes an anthem of public proclamation from which no one - no one - is excluded and for which no risk is too great. True discipleship, we know from the life of the Christ whom we follow, is not membership in a clerical social club called a church. That is not an ordination that the truly ordained can abide.

Discipleship is not an intellectual exercise or assent to a body of doctrine. True discipleship is an attitude of mind, a quality of soul, a way of living that is not political but which has serious political implications, and that may not be officially ecclesiastical but which, in the end, will change a church that is more ecclesiastical than communal. Real discipleship changes things because it simply cannot ignore things as they are. It refuses anything and everything that defies the will of God for humanity ... no matter how sensible, no matter how rational, no matter how common, no matter how obvious, no matter how historically patriarchal, no matter how often it has been called "The will of God" by those who purport to determine what that is or intend to impose on others what they say it is. The disciple takes public issue with the values of a world that advantages only those who are already advantaged. The true disciple takes aim at institutions that call themselves "freeing" but which keep half the people of the world in bondage. It takes umbrage at systems that are more bent on keeping improper people out of them than they are in welcoming all people into them. True discipleship takes the side always, always, always of the poor, the minority, the outcast, the reviled, the rejected, the other, despite the power of the rich and powerful - not because the poor and powerless are more virtuous than the rich and powerful but because the God of love wills for them, too, what the rich and powerful debate or refuse for them.

Discipleship cuts a reckless path through corporation types like Herod; through institution types like the Pharisees, through system types like the money-changers, and through chauvinist types like apostles who want to send women away. Discipleship stands bare naked in the middle of the world's marketplace and, in the name of Jesus, cries aloud all the cries of the world until someone, somewhere hears and responds to the poorest of the poor, the lowest of the low, the most outcast of the rejected. Anything else - all the pomp, all the gold lace and red silk, all the rituals in the world - the gospels attest, is certainly mediocre and surely bogus discipleship.

And therein lies the problem: it is one thing, then, for an individual to summon the courage it takes to stand alone in the eye of a storm called "The real world." It is another thing entirely to see the church itself be anything less than a true reflection of the living Christ. Why? Because the church of Jesus Christ may not be called to ordained priesthood as we know it now, but the church of Christ is always, undoubtedly, surely called to true discipleship. For the church - for you and me then, as well as the institution - not to meet what discipleship demands now is for the church to abandon the discipleship it demands the world to pursue. To see a church of Christ deny the poor and the outcast their due, institute the very systems in itself what it despises in society, is to see no church at all. It is at best religion reduced to one more social institution designed to comfort the comfortable but not to challenge the chains that bind most of humanity - and all of its women - to the cross. In this kind of church, the gospel has been long reduced to the catechism. In this kind of church, prophecy dies and justice whimpers and the truth becomes too dim for the searching heart to see.

Today, as never before in history, perhaps, the world and therefore the church within it, is being stretched to the breaking point by life situations that, if for no other reason than their immensity are shaking the globe to its foundations. New life questions are emerging with startling impact and relentless persistence. And the greatest of them all is the woman's question.

Women are most of the poor, most of the refugees, most of the uneducated, most of the beaten, most of the rejected of the world. Even in the church where educated, dedicated, committed women are ignored even in the pronouns of the Mass! Where is the presence of Jesus to the beaten woman, to the beggar woman, to the abandoned woman, to the woman alone, to the woman whose questions, cries and life experience have no place in the systems of the world and no place in the church either? Except of course, to be defined as a second kind of human nature, not quite as competent, not quite as valued, not quite as human, not quite as graced by God as men are?

The real question must be the third one. What does the theology of discipleship demand here? What does the theology of a priestly people imply here? Are women simply half a disciple of Christ? To be half commissioned, half noticed, and half valued? In the light of these situations, there are, consequently, questions in the Christian community today that cannot be massaged by footnotes nor obscured by jargon nor made palatable by the retreat to "faith." On the contrary, before these issues, the footnotes falter. Church language itself serves only to heighten the question and faith itself demands the question. The discipleship of women is the question that is not going to go away, however much they pray it will or legislate it into ecclesiastical obscurity. Indeed, the discipleship of the church in regard to women is the question that will, in the long run, prove the church itself. In the woman's question the church is facing one of its most serious challenges to discipleship since the emergence of the slavery question when we argued then, too, that slavery was the will of God for some people - but not us.

The major question facing Christians today, perhaps, is what does discipleship mean in a church that doesn't want women anywhere except in the pews. If discipleship is reduced to maleness, what does that do to the rest of the Christian dispensation? If only men can really live discipleship to the fullest, what is the use of a woman aspiring to the discipleship baptism implies, demands, demonstrates in the life of Jesus at all? What does it mean for the women themselves who are faced with rejection, devaluation, and a debatable theology based on the remnants of a bad biology theologized? What do we do when a church proclaims the equality of women but builds itself on structures that assure their inequality? What as well does the rejection of women at the highest levels of the church mean for men who claim to be enlightened but continue to support the very system that mocks half the human race? What does it mean for the church that claims to be a follower of the Jesus who healed on the Sabbath and raised women from the dead and contended with the teachers of the faith - mandatum or no mandatum, "definitive" documents or no definitive documents. And finally, what does it mean for a society badly in need of a cosmic worldview on the morning of a global age?

The answers are discouragingly clear on all counts. Christian discipleship is not simply in danger of being stunted. Discipleship has, in fact, become the enemy. Who we do not want to admit to full, official, legitimated discipleship - something the church itself teaches is required of us all - has become at least as problematic for the integrity of the church as the exclusion of women from those deliberations of the church that shape its theology and form its people. Women are beginning to wonder if discipleship has anything to do with them at all. And therein lies the contemporary question, the present challenge of discipleship. Some consider faithfulness to the gospel to mean doing what we have always done. Others find faithfulness only in being what we have always been. The distinction is crucial to our understanding of tradition. The distinction is also essential to the understanding of discipleship in the modern church. When "the tradition" becomes synonymous with "the system" and maintaining the system becomes more important than maintaining the spirit of the tradition, discipleship shrivels and becomes at best "obedience" or "fidelity" to the past but not deep-down commitment to the presence of the living Christ confronting the leprosies of the age.

Ancient society called the blind sinful, a female child useless, a menstruating woman unclean, all of them marginal to the system, condemned to the fringes of life, excluded from the center of the synagogue, barred from the heart of the temple. But Jesus takes each of them to himself, despite the laws, regardless of the culture, notwithstanding the disapproval of the spiritual notables of the area and fills them with himself and sends them as himself out to the highways and byways of the entire world. To be disciples of Jesus means that we must do the same. There are some things, it seems, that brook no rationalizing for the sake of institutional niceties. Discipleship infers, implies, requires no less than the confirming rdaining love of Jesus for everyone, every-where regardless of who would dare to take upon themselves the audacious right to draw limits around the will of God for those we call unlovable. To define 'faith' as willingness to accept the unacceptable is faith bereft of Jesus.

Discipleship and faith are of a piece. To say that we believe that God loves the poor, judges in their behalf, wills their deliverance but do nothing ourselves to free the poor, to hear their pleas, lift their burdens, to act in their behalf is an empty faith indeed.. To say that God is love and not ourselves love as God loves may well be church but it is not Christianity. To preach a theology of equality, to say that all persons are equal in God's sight but at the same time maintain a theology of inequality, a spirituality of domination, that bars half the human race on the basis of gender from the fullness of faith, that says that women have no place in the dominion of the church and the development of doctrine - and all of this in the name of God is to live a lie.

But if discipleship is the following of Jesus, beyond all boundaries, at all costs, for the bringing of the reign of God, for the establishment of right relationships, then to ground a woman's calling to follow Christ on her inability to look like Jesus obstructs the very thing the church is founded to do. It obstructs a woman's ability to follow Christ to the full, to give her life for the others, to bless and preach and sacrifice and build community "in his name" - as the documents on priesthood say that a priestly people must and it does it for the sake of religion in defiance of the gospel itself.

How can a church such as this call convincingly to the world in the name of justice to practice a justice it does not practice itself. How is it that the church can call other institutions to deal with women as full human beings made in the image of God when their humanity is precisely what the church itself holds against them in the name of God.

It is a philosophical question of immense proportions. It is the question which, like slavery, brings the church to the test. For the church to be present to the woman's question, to minister to it, to be disciple to it, the church must itself become converted to the issue, in fact, the church must become converted by the issue. Men who do not take the woman's issue seriously may be priests but they cannot possibly be disciples. They cannot possibly be 'Other Christs.' Not the Christ born of a woman. Not the Christ who commissioned women to preach him. Not the Christ who took faculties from a woman at Cana. Not the Christ who sent women to preach resurrection and redemption of the flesh to apostles who would not believe it then and do not believe it now. Not the Christ who sent the Holy Spirit on Mary the woman as well as on Peter the man. Not the Christ who announced his messiahship as clearly to the Samaritan woman as to the rock that shattered. If this is the Jesus whom we as Christians, as church, are to follow, then the discipleship of the church is now mightily in question.

Indeed, the poet Basho writes: "I do not seek to follow in the footsteps of those of old. I seek the things they sought." Discipleship depends on our bringing the will of God for humankind to the questions of this age as Jesus did to his. As long as tradition is used to mean following in the footsteps of our past rather than seeking to maintain the spirit of the Christ in the present, then it is unlikely that we will preserve more than the shell of the church.

The consciousness of the universalism of humanity across differences has become the thread that binds the world together in a global age. What was once a hierarchy of humankind is coming to be seen for what it is: the oppression of humankind. The colonization of women is coming to be seen as unacceptable now as the colonial oppression of Africa, the crusades against Turks, the enslavement of Blacks and the decimation of indigenous peoples in the name of God.

It is true that theological debates are raging everywhere; but it is also true that everywhere the Holy Spirit is breaking through - as the Holy Spirit did in Rome in the 60's. In Asia, Buddhist women are demanding ordination and the right to make the sacred mandalas. In India, women are beginning to do the sacred dances and light the sacred fires. In Judaism, women study Torah and now carry the scrolls and read the scriptures and lead the congregations. Only in the most backward, most legalistic, most primitive of cultures are women made invisible, made useless, made less than fully human, less than fully spiritual. The humanization of the human race is upon us. The only question for the church is whether the humanization of the human race will lead as well to the Christianization of the Christian church. Otherwise, discipleship will die and the integrity of the church with it.

We must take discipleship seriously or we shall leave the church of the future with functionaries but without disciples. We cannot renew priesthood without renewing discipleship - our own as well as others. The fact is that Christianity lives in Christians, not in books, not in documents called 'definitive' to hide the fact that they are at best time-bound, not in platitudes about "special vocations," not in old errors, dignified as "tradition." The new fact of life is that discipleship to women and the discipleship of women is key to the discipleship of the rest of the church.

The questions are clear. The answer is obscure and uncertain but crucial to the future, of a church that claims to be eternal. Thomas Carlyle wrote, "Our main business is not to see what lies dimly in the distance, but to do what lies clearly at hand." A group such as this, you, at a time such as this - a priestly people in a priestless period - must keep the total vision, the final vision, the ultimate vision, the inevitable vision - cleanly in mind. Yes. But we must also keep the tasks of the present clearly in mind and the task of the present is not simply preparation for priestly ordination in a church intent on obstructing it, that either doubts - or fears - the power of the truth to persuade and so denies the right even to discuss this festering question of whether or not women can participate in the sacrament of orders. Clearly, preparation for ordination to the priesthood would be premature, at best, if not downright damaging to the Spirit itself in a climate such as this. No, the task of the present in a time such as this is to use every organization to which we belong to develop the theology of the church to a point of critical mass.

The task now is to practice a dangerous discipleship. We need a group free of mandatums that will organize seminars, hold public debates in the style of the great medieval disputations that argued for and against the full humanity of indigenous peoples, hold teach-ins, sponsor publications, write books, post educational web sites, hold more and more gatherings like this one where women speak freely no matter what happens to anyone participating in them.. We must gather groups around the topics of the infallibility of infallibility and the role of the 'sensus fidelium' in the development of doctrine, and the question of the clear exclusion of women from the restoration of the permanent diaconate - an official manner of discipleship for women that has theology, history, ritual, liturgy and tradition firmly, fully and clearly on its side.

It is time to bring into the light of day the discussions that lurk behind every church door, in every seeking heart. If as Vatican II says, priesthood requires preaching, sacrifice and community building, then proclaiming the coming of a new church, sacrificing ourselves to bring it, and shaping a community new with the notion of a new kind of priest and permanent woman deacons may be the greatest priestly service of them all right now.

So, like the old lady, we must keep turning, turning, turning in the direction of discipleship - as women always have - but differently now. For as Basho says, we do not seek to follow in the footsteps of those of old. We seek the things they sought. We don't seek to do what they really need. We need to do much more than that. We need now to do what they really, really need. Why? Because as John XXIII says in 'Pacem in Terris', "Whenever people discover that they have rights, they have the responsibility to claim them." And because Proverbs teaches clearly, "If the people will lead, the leaders will eventually follow." Therefore, what must we do now as priestly people? We must take responsibility. We must take back the church. We must lead leaders to the fullness of Christian life!

* * *

24

We will pour our ointment on the feet of the church

Ecumenical Movement and the Ordination of Women!

Aruna Gnanadason

(Aruna Gnanadason, a recognised Asian Woman theologian has been attached to the WCC as Coordinator of the Women's Programme since 1991.She is the author of: The Church and Violence Against Women(WCC publishers) and co-edited: Women,Violence and Non-Violent change and was supposed to give the Keynote Speech at the Dublin Conference. As she had to drop out at the last moment due to various pressures, she circulated her prepared speech, which is given below. ed.)

In this paper I focus on the ecumenical discussion on this issue, from the perspective of women of World Council of Churches' membership who have been wrestling with the issue in their own churches. As I read books, articles and personal testimonies to prepare this paper, I was amazed how many times women spoke of their pain but also of their joy as they encouraged their churches to recognise the spiritual and pastoral gifts they have to offer.

But first an anecdote. I.R.H. Gnanadason my father-in-law was a Bishop of the Church of South India and Moderator of the Church, when he died in 1973. He has been widely acknowledged as one of the greatest Bishops the Church has had in its almost 55 year history as a United Church. He died before my son was born but it was his memory that my son honoured when he was just 5 years old as I was trying to get him ready for school. He said, "I don't need to go to school, or to study because when I grow up I am going to become a Bishop like *thatha (grandfather)*, and for this schooling is not necessary. To be a Bishop, all I need to know is about God. And I already know about God."

The more I thought about what he said, the more it made sense. Ordained ministry is about a calling, it is about the courage to "give oneself to the Church in utter devotion" - it is indeed about "knowing" God. Therefore it follows that anyone - woman or man - who feels called to this ministry and comes to that conviction with humility and utter devotion to God, to the vocation of priesthood and to the community, deserves to have that call tested and be ordained as a priest of the church. Such a call needs to be tested against the communities' needs, it is not simply an individual's personal desire - it requires the embracing support of a community, which discerns the Spirit leading them.

Making a difference

My church has ordained women as priests for the past 25 years, and one of the "stories" of ordained women is that of Nirmala Vasanthakumar, one of the first two women ordained by the Church of South India. She along with her husband shared ministry in a congregation. She speaks of an incident when a woman who brought her child for baptism asked that she be baptised by Nirmala rather than her husband, because as a woman she would understand better what it means to give birth and nurture a child.

A year after the first women were ordained by the Church of England in 1994, a magazine commented: "Approximately a year ago, 38 women were ordained in the Church of England. In 1995, the total is more than 1400, constituting one-tenth of clergy in that

church. The Anglicans have observed an increase in religious practice in parishes where a woman priest officiates ... the number of
parishioners increased by between 10 to 30 percent following the
calling of a woman to serve as parish priest."

In other words, women priests can make a difference. It is true
that for some churches the problem is theological - but other
churches are re-examining the heart of their faith and have found
theological and spiritual resources and insights, which have led
them to ordain women. At the same time, I would state clearly,
right away, that in this process we as women need to contribute to
a redefining, refining and reconstructing of what priesthood is all
about. We need to constantly challenge those who would still hold
on to an understanding of the clergy "as an authoritarian sacerdo-
tal caste with only formal ties to a community."

We live in a world of exclusion and violence; a world with un-
told forms of discrimination that threaten the integrity of communities; a world that constantly poses difficult moral and ethical choices
to men and women; a world where secular forces are strong and
spirituality is undermined; a world where religious fundamentalism
runs rife and religion is used to legitimise communal identities leading to conflicts. Additionally, in the life of the church itself, increasingly there is evidence of gender based discrimination and even of
sexual abuse of women in pastoral contexts and more recently of
the new steps the church has been called to take in the face of
increasing evidence of paedophilia. In such a context, what should
ordained ministry be about? The Church is called to respond with
compassion and pastoral fortitude. At the heart of the commitment to the ordination of women and men must be the concern for
the community in which the church is present to serve. Therefore,
women in ordained ministry must be viewed within the framework
of, "partnership or community rather than in isolation, because of
the desperate needs of the people and the earth. Everywhere one
turns there is reconciliation to be made, bodily and emotional

wounds to be healed, relationships to be righted, wrongs to be amended and simple acknowledgements to be made." Ordained ministry of women can be a "way to subvert the church into being the church", as Letty Russell describes it. She says this in the context of her own experience as an ordained woman for 35 years as the minister of a poor community church in East Harlem.

And as we discuss this issue, we are surrounded by a crowd of witnesses, women saints ancient and new who have been recognised by the church for the spiritual gifts they offer to the church - a "priesthood" of love, care and compassion that they have through the centuries offered to the church and human communities they served. They stand as our spiritual guides as we discuss this question. While the tradition of sainthood has been on the edges of the Protestant traditions and has accompanied us in our liturgical life, it is the Orthodox Tradition that has offered this gift to the ecumenical movement. As we know, among the saints are a number of women saints, often, ordinary women who worked uncompromisingly and sacrificially for Christ and their communities. Ion Bria, Romanian Orthodox theologian describes the ministry of the saints to the Church in this way: "The faithful are called saints because of their participation in the holiness of God, who is holy by nature (Isa. 6:3), in Christ (Phil.4:21). They are "God's chosen ones, holy (or saints)" (Col. 3:12). One aspect of the mystery of the church is this new consecration in Christ of a "kingdom of priests", "consecrated nation", "royal priesthood" (Ex. 19: 6; Isa. 43: 20-21; I Pet. 2: 9) which is not exclusive or restricted. This among other things is the tradition that has inspired women in the Orthodox Church to begin discussions on the ordination of women to the priesthood in their churches, which I refer to later in this paper.

On April 1 this year, I was privileged to witness the consecration of the third woman Bishop of the Lutheran Church in Germany, Bishop Barbel Wartenberg Potter who had designed most of the liturgy for the ceremony herself. The most moving part of the afternoon was the time for the laying on of hands. Among those who laid their hands on her to bless her, Bishop Maria Jepsen and Bishop Margot Kaessmann, the other two women bishops in Germany, along with male bishops from German churches and bishops from Africa, Papua New Guinea, Latvia, India and the United Kingdom. But there was also Marie Dilger a housewife and friend of Bishop Wartenberg Potter. All of them invoked the Holy Spirit to lead her on in her ministry. The new Bishop was not only received into the Lutheran Church of Holstein-Lübeck, but she was received into the community of the church, a global community, a community that goes beyond ecclesial boundaries. She starts her ministry with manifold blessings - the blessings of God, the blessings of the community and the blessings of women. The words and a garland of flowers offered by the women of the Diocese symbolised this last. This ceremony came after her formal election and approval of her election by the women and men of that diocese. Her community or "her congregation" were in prayer with her, as she acknowledged her servant-hood to them.

Call or Vocation

Most women who are ordained and those who are in dialogue with their churches on the issue of the ordination of women would speak of how they have been called to this vocation. Some women are concerned that the church abuses the concept of the call as a way of "keeping women in their place" - ecclesial authorities tell women that they are called to diaconal or other ministries and not to priesthood. Nancy Duff writes that, "The doctrine of vocation affirms that every individual life with its unique combination of gifts and limitations has divinely appointed purpose and that we are called to glorify God in all we do." She continues later in the same text, "Although the doctrine of vocation can be misused to counsel tolerance for oppressive situations, if rightly interpreted it challenges oppressive conditions." With women there is a difference in their understanding of the calling. In India for instance, many women enter theological schools, as a first choice, fully aware that they have no guarantee of ordination, or even of a job, and even if their churches will ordain them, they have no assurance that local congregations will accept them as priests. They enter anyway, with the conviction that it is their vocation, a call they cannot ignore.

In a collection of personal testimonies, on Women in the Ministry, every woman who has contributed refers to her ordination as a response to her vocation. Some of these voices: Alison Fuller of the Scottish Episcopal Church speaks of the denial of her vocation by the Church as the denial of women's humanity before God; Elizabeth Wardlaw of the Church of Scotland compares her vocation, her calling to that of Paul on the road to Damascus; Margaret Forrester ordained by the United Reformed Church speaks of being aware "of an overpowering sense of vocation which every church in which I worshipped had refused to recognise. The frustration and pain of this were hard to bear." Jean Mayland of the Church of England writes: "I had come to believe that I had a vocation to the priesthood when I was in my teens, but of course I was told this was completely impossible. I was brought up in a high Anglo Catholic church where my faith was nurtured and my vocation spurned".

Taking the risk responding to the call

"The Church will never believe that women have a religious message until some of them get and take the opportunity to prove they have." - Maude Royden

Let us follow just one of the women quoted earlier. Jean Mayland, one of the first women ordained by the Church of England, shares her struggles and joys in the process leading to her ordination and what followed. In 1907, the Anglican Church ordained the first woman, Li Tim Oi a Chinese woman, in Xingxing, in China. From there it has slowly but surely spread - to Hong Kong, USA, Canada, New Zealand, Latin America, Kenya and other African countries, the united Church of South India and Ireland. In 1862, the Order of the Deaconesses was revived in the Anglican Church and Elizabeth Ferrar was ordained as the first deaconess.

Jean Mayland describes how she pursued her vocation: "During my theology year I went for a selection conference and was accepted to train as a 'Lady Worker' in the Church of England. On reflection I felt I could not face all the limitations and frustrations that would be involved in that work. I felt called to priesthood and not to 'lady worker ship'. I do so admire those women who moved in and worked as 'lady/women workers', and later as deaconesses. With courage and patience they pushed back the boundaries. I could not have done it. I would either have exploded or have been destroyed and embittered by frustration."

And so she got into the fray and with other women accompanied her church on the way to the final decision to ordain women. She speaks of how she, "along with my sister priests, have had to campaign and also fight with our church long and hard. Yet I love the Church of England with every fibre of my being... ". In 1992, she was one of the few privileged women, (having won in the ballot for tickets) to be able to sit in the gallery of the Church House and witness the debate and final approval of ordination of women to priesthood. She reminiscences, "I managed to overcome my urge to burst into tears, and expressed my joy and delight that after all these years this had happened.... The words that came to my mind were those of Siegfried Sassoon's poem about Armistice Day, which concludes 'and the singing will never be done.'"

But, there was not much space for singing after that - things did not go with the smoothness women hoped for. The press, which wanted to sensationalise the news about the ordination, especially because there was enough awareness of the opposition to it, constantly misquoted her. Some of the Bishops and senior staff seemed to be more concerned about keeping in the church those who opposed the ordination, than to celebrate with the women their success. Even deans and canons showed their hostility. Family obligations did not make life easier. She was not able to take up frill time ministry. While the earlier quotation from a magazine indicates that the ordained women in the Anglican Church of England did bring change in some congregations, it is also true that a few years after the decision to ordain women, many did not get parish ministries, they had to go into specialised areas of work of the church or accept Assistant posts.

But Jean Mayland was one of the 38 women to be ordained in that first batch. She writes: "I am eternally grateful to God, with whom I often wrestle, that along the mysterious path of life where the going is often so dark, She has brought me on occasions to sit in places of stimulation, or of tranquillity and joy" She speaks of the deep emotions she experienced the first time she celebrated the Eucharist, "When I began the Eucharistic Prayer I felt I would not be able to get through it without collapsing into tears.... Never will leading the people in making Eucharist lose its humbling thrill, but never again will it be such an awe-inspiring privilege as that first time."

I have traced the struggles and joys of one woman in one member church of the WCC who has gone through such a history because it is these women we have at the centre of our thoughts, when we speak of the ordination of women. One meets women like Jean Mayland in every part of the world - women who so love the church that they are willing to put their lives and those of their families on the line, for the sake of what they believe in intensely. Women who follow for whom ordination is now a given, will never be able to fathom what price their "fore-sisters and mothers" have paid. The Team Visits to the member churches of the World Council of Churches at the mid-point of the Ecumenical Decade of the Churches in Solidarity with Women, met with women in many churches where this is an issue. The report of the team visits, the

Living Letters records that: "There are churches in all regions which forbid the ordination of women, even where they can cite no doctrinal or theological reasons why this should be so. While some churches recognise women's gifts, many are quite slow and even resistant to recognise and support women in ministry. Even where women have - after much struggle - been trained and ordained, fair pay, stable placements and moral support as they exercise their ministry are not guaranteed to them. After graduation many women ministers must wait a long time to receive a posting. They may be forced to chose between vocation and family."

The challenge to the ecumenical movement....

The women I speak of here are all from the World Council of Churches' membership churches and from the constituency the World Council of Churches (WCC) serves. At the Decade Festival (Harare, Zimbabwe, November 1998) that brought to conclusion the Decade a letter was addressed to WCC Assembly. In what I consider, was a regrettable mistake the issue of the ordination of women is referred to as "an ethical and theological problem" for the church. The drafters of the text left it this way to respect women from churches where ordination of women is not yet an issue. Strong, requests from ordained women present that this formulation be changed, and a new paragraph be drafted devoted to just the question of ordination, to highlight both their joys and difficulties, was ignored. The process did not allow for their voices to be heard and this left many women who had been involved in long years of struggle for ordination to the priesthood, disillusioned and unsatisfied. This has convinced the WCC of the need for further discussion on the ordination of women was evident and discussions have begun within the Faith and Order Commission (of which the Roman Catholic Church is an official member) to re-engage the member churches on this issue.

The question of ordination of women and the unity of the Church

"Openness to each other holds the possibility that the Spirit may well speak to one church through the insights of another"(Baptism, Eucharist and Ministry text)

That the issue of the ordination of women has been one of the most divisive of issues for the churches has to be acknowledged. Mary Tanner, former Moderator of the Faith and Order Commission of the World Council of Churches, describes the dilemma clearly when she writes that among the churches that grew out of the Reformation, the movement to ordain women to full ministry of word and sacrament, "coincided with the movement towards the visible unity of the church. The one has had an effect on the other. This result is not surprising, for the visible unity of the church involves the recognition not only of all its baptized members as members of a single community of faith but also of those who are called to be ministers of one communion." She quotes Anglican Archbishop William Temple who expressed the view, as early as 1916, which she says has been shared by many other committed ecumenists, "I would like to see women ordained.... desirable as it would be in itself, the effect might be (probably would be) to put back the re-union of Christendom - and reunion is more important."

While the question of the ordination of women is certainly not easily given the diversity of positions among the various church traditions that are part of the ecumenical movement, whether the question of the ordination of women can be held responsible for the slow and arduous process to visible unity is a matter of debate. But there are several instances where the issue did affect unity discussions: the Anglicans did not join in the United Church of Canada in 1956 because that church ordained women. In the Anglican-Methodist unity scheme in England in the 1960's the

Methodists delayed the ordination of women till it was obvious that the unity scheme had failed. Even in the covenanting process that followed involving the United Reformed Church, the Methodists, the Moravian and the Anglican churches, the ordination of women once again was an issue. The Church of England included a separate motion referring to the recognition of women ministers of other churches - this was defeated in the House of Clergy. At the Consultation of united and uniting churches in 1987, the situation was summed up this way: "For some churches the ordination of women adds to the hindrances to unity; but the united churches are clear that further union for them is being made a more open possibility by the willingness of those to share the ordination of women which they have found to be a creative element in their common life."

According to Mary Tanner: "The contribution of the WCC has been to help the churches to set the discussion within the context of an emerging convergence on the understanding of ministry and priesthood and, perhaps even more important, within the concept of the unity we seek. The studies on the unity of the church and the renewal of human community have enlarged and enriched the perspective of this unity. Some have come to maintain that the churches' ministry must include women in order to show to the world the depths of unity in human community and make the gospel and the vision of the kingdom credible in a broken and divided world. The unity of the church ought not to be set over against the unity of the human community."

Melanie May had posed a similar question when she asked, "At the end, each and everyone of us will need to search our hearts before God to discern whether we believe with Archbishop William Temple that visible church unity is "more important" than the ordination of women or whether visible church unity is at all achievable unless all baptized members - men and women alike in God's image - can fulfill the ministry to which God has called them in Christ."

Preceding the formation of the World Council of Churches, at the very first World Conference on Faith and Order in 1927 in Lausanne, of the 400 church delegates only 7 were women and yet they issued a prophetic motion which was accepted by that body. It is recorded in the Minutes: "the right place of women in the Church is one of grave moment and should be in the hearts and minds of all." Commenting on this Lukas Vischer writes, "They pointed out that if the Church seeks deeper unity it must re-examine the question of the relationship between women and men, and that the mission task makes it imperative to put to better use all the gifts available in the Church. They deliberately refrained from raising the problem of church order in this connection. But already at that time it was clear that it would not be possible to avoid facing the question later."

The Third Assembly of the WCC in New Delhi, in 1961, called on the Working Committee on Faith and Order "to establish a study on the theological, biblical and ecclesiological issues involved in the ordination of women". It was also stressed that the study be undertaken in close conjunction with the Department on Cooperation of Men and Women in Church, Family and Society. The Working Committee of the Faith and Order approved the proposal and decided to place the question of ordination of women on the agenda of the Fourth World Conference on Faith and Order to be held in Montreal, Canada in July 1963

"This decision was felt as necessary because the problem is of practical concern to an increasing number of churches. Many churches welcome women to the ordained ministry and have found the policy advantageous. Others, having adopted this policy, face serious tensions. In others, the policy is under discussion and provokes heated debate. The matter frequently becomes acute in negotiations for church unity. And even apart from formal negotiations, it affects the mutual relations of churches that ordain women to those that do not. It would be wrong, therefore, to view this issue as a result of feminist demands or agitation by a few enthusiasts. It concerns the total understanding of the ministry of the church and therefore has deep theological significance."

This position spoken of nearly 40 years ago remains true till today, though in this period many churches have decided to and have ordained women to priesthood. It continues to be regrettable that some churches even today, view this deep longing of women to respond to their vocation as a campaign of a few feminists making unreasonable demands!

Two other important contributions to the discussion

In the work of the Faith and Order Commission, there were two other important study processes that have contributed to the ongoing discussions on the ordination of women. The first is the Community of Women and Men Study process that had been initiated during the V Assembly of the WCC in Nairobi in 1975 and which culminated in 1981 at an international consultation in Sheffield. This process was based on a recognition that "the unity of the church requires that women be free to live out the gifts that God has given them and to respond to their calling to share fully in the life and witness of the church." The process was to be an ecclesiological study, focused on the recognition that 'women's issues' are issues concerning the wholeness of the whole church, a study of church unity with particular regards to the experience of women. As a result, "Significant ecclesiological challenges emerging from the study included questions about the structures of the church, about how power and authority were exercised and by whom. The question of power and exclusive leadership inevitably brought up the controversial questions of the ordination of women to the priesthood and the episcopate. Although there was no agreement on the answers to these questions, at Sheffield they were clearly, and often painfully, articulated."

At Sheffield the discussion recognised "the complexity and diversity of the existing situations both within and between the different churches. The state of the discussion is also at different stages in different cultures. Amongst the churches there is a plurality of practice embracing those who do ordain women, those who do not, and those who are hesitant for ecumenical reasons" The report goes on to say that as knowledge of theology and sociology develop, "we are offered a chance to deepen our understanding and practice of ministry and our relations with one another... The issues involved in this matter touch us at our deepest level, embedded as they are in liturgy, symbolism and spirituality. There can be no real progress if church, state or any group within the church seeks to force a change in practice without taking this into account." Sheffield also pointed to the fact that the problems of the ministry are related "to the social and cultural context where the identity of the church and individual Christians is being constantly challenged."

It is important to comment here that at that time it was assumed that the ordination of women was an issue of concern only for women from western protestant churches. But women from all parts of the world have described their own struggles with their churches. They have challenged their churches for reverting to cultural contexts in their societies as the base for excluding women. Musimbi Kanyoro gathers together some of these voices from Asia, Africa and Latin America in the book entitled In Search of a Round Table. She writes about African women: "....the powers of healing, preaching and spiritual direction, typically understood by the Christian Church to be priestly duties, are powers traditionally exercised by women and men in African societies. If there is to be any general picture of African women in ordained ministries, an inclusive study of the religious roles played by women in different types of societies in Africa is imperative." Datuk Thu En-Yu from Malaysia makes a similar claim about women's roles in societies, which follow the path of Buddhism, Taoism and Confucianism.

Baptism, Eucharist and Ministry Document ... another opportunity?

The second important stream in the WCC was the study, which culminated in Lima, Peru in January 1982, where the Faith and Order Commission gave final form to a convergence text entitled Baptism. Eucharist and Ministry (BEM) for discussion in the churches. It marked points of "theological convergence among the churches on issues which traditionally caused division among the churches." It was at this same meeting that the final report of the Community Study was also received. However, the BEM document does not treat the ordination of women to priesthood in the main part of the ministry text but considers the issue in a commentary that gives a short description of the positions of churches that ordain women and those that do not.

Janet Crawford feels that the BEM text was not entirely uninfluenced by the Community Study. She writes: "In both the baptism and eucharist sections of the text there are 'theological insights about unity, equality and the imaging of Christ in us all' which, at least implicitly, makes connections to the community study and which may signal to women that they are 'partners in the search for the visible unity of the church.' "It is in the section on ministry that the lack of connection between BEM and the Community Study becomes most obvious. The whole controversial issue of the ordination of women is dealt with in two carefully formulated and balanced paragraphs which conclude that: 'An increasing number of churches have decided that there is no biblical or theological reason against ordaining women, and many of them have subsequently proceeded to do so. Yet many churches hold that the tradition of the church in this regard must not be changed.' (BEM, "Ministry" para 18)"

Commenting on the BEM text, Crawford quotes Cardman: ". . . in the much-praised Lima text itself, little attention has been paid to what was described as 'the most obvious point of present and potential disagreement, namely, the ordination of women'. (Cardman, BEM and the Community of Women and Men Study, Journal of Ecumenical Studies, 21 Winter 1988). Rather, on this point it seemed that Faith and Order nad retreated from its bolder statements. The result satisfied neither opponents nor proponents of women's ordination, and did little to advance dialogue between the two. BEM gave no lead to the vital and church-dividing question of women's ordination."

Respecting diversity.... the key to mutuality and ecumenical discipline

Women too come into this discussion from different understandings and from varying positions. This diversity has to be respected, because clearly the ecumenical movement among women does not intend to call for any one uniform pattern of ordained ministry. Even in those churches where it is still not openly discussed women are beginning to discuss the issue. While there are many examples of World council of Churches member churches I can reflect on, I refer here to the contributions of Orthodox Christian women to the discussion. Three important books that have been offered by Orthodox women theologians are: Elisabeth Behr-Sigel's *The Ministry of Women in the Church* published first in French in 1987 (Oakwood Publications, California); Kyriaki Karidoyanes Fitzgerald's *Women Deacons in the Orthodox Church, Called to Holiness and Ministry* published in 1998 and revised and republished in 1999 (Holy Cross Orthodox Press, Massachusetts); and Elisabeth Behr-Sigel and Kallistos Ware's *The Ordination of Women in the Orthodox Church* published in 2000 (World Council of Churches, Geneva).

A series of meetings of Orthodox women - all under the patronage of the leadership of the Orthodox churches - starting with the first in Agapia, Romania in 1976; Rhodes in 1988; Damascus 1996 and Istanbul, 1997 - all have addressed this issue. Some of the participants in the meeting in Damascus welcomed "the idea of organising an inter-Orthodox conference on the ordination of women to the priesthood.". Orthodox Christian women have participated in ecumenical women's meetings and would naturally be influenced by the discussions. But Behr-Sigel refers to the new challenges within the Orthodox Churches themselves and describes one of the signs of the times as "a call that we should discern between the living Tradition and a fossilized traditionalism, particularly regarding the place of women.". She writes: "As responsible theologians in the Orthodox Church - both men and women - have become aware of these contradictions, the question of the admission of women to a sacramental ministry has arisen. The question no longer comes to them only from outside in the course of ecumenical dialogue, but it has also become for them an internal problem."

The World Council of Churches offers an ecumenical space...

The impact of the Community of Women and Men Study and the theological and anthropological challenges it posed; the Ecumenical Decade of the Churches in Solidarity with Women and the unfinished ecclesiological challenges it has left the churches with and the newly begun process Being Church: Women's Voices and Visions which will explore the ways in which women vision the Church and its forms of leadership and ministries - all will leave an indelible mark on the churches and their search for visible unity. All these processes will contribute to the proposed Faith and Order, consultation on "Ministry and Ordination in the Community of Women and Men" to be held in 2002, which will certainly contribute to this discussion. The decision to hold such a conference was taken by the Faith and Order Board at its meeting held in Toronto, Canada in June 1999. Introducing the debate Melanie May, spoke of how the 'Discussion on the Ordination of women is threaded through the ecumenical movement in the 20th century. This thread of discussion is, however, a slender one and has, at times, been all but unraveled by silence on the subject. Today we seek to weave this thread more integrally into the search for visible unity of the Church, acknowledging that the visible unity of the Church is predicated on the recognition of all baptized members and the recognition of all those called to ordained ministries. We cannot, therefore, achieve the visible unity of the Church, unless we are willing to walk together, in truth and love, about the question of women's ministries, including the ordination of women."

Are we willing to walk together in truth and love in our search for unity? This is the question that accompanies the WCC and its designing of the concept of an "ecumenical space" to provide a safe environment for difficult and church dividing issues, such as the ordination of women, to be discussed.

Konrad Raiser, General Secretary in his report to the VIII Assembly of the WCC in Harare, 1998 said, "In the uncertainty of the present situation, with its temptation to see identity in a defensive and exclusive way, the ecumenical movement needs to recapture the sense of the pilgrim people of God, of churches on the way together, ready to transcend the boundaries of their history and tradition, listening together to the voice of the Shepherd, recognizing and resonating with each other as those energized by the same Spirit. The World Council of Churches, as a fellowship of churches, marks the space where such risky encounter can take place, where confidence and trust can be built and community can grow. At present, this conviction is being tested severely by conflicts over moral issues, especially regarding human sexuality, and by the ecclesiological and theological challenges arising from the Ecumenical Decade of the Churches in Solidarity with Women. More than ever before we need the WCC as an ecumenical space which is open and yet embraced by the faithfulness of God and protected by the bond of peace, a space of mutual acceptance and understanding as well as of mutual challenge and correction."

In the discussion on the ordination of women within this ecumenical space, the most important criteria will be to discern the diversity of voices and opinions on the issue and to enter the discussion with sensitivity and respect for different ecclesiologies. It requires all parties to listen attentively to each other - to listen to the struggles over vocation. It is critical that in unity talks where "churches which take a more traditional view are contemplating union with churches which believe that in ordaining women they are led by the Spirit", that the churches participating "seriously face the theological issues involved", and in this "it is much to be hoped that whatever decision an individual church reaches there will be no accusation of heresy but that its decision will be accepted by others as a genuine effort to follow the guidance of the Holy Spirit." Additionally, we cannot undertake our discussion of the ordination of women or the ordination of men without serious and sustained discussion of the ministry of all baptised members and the fact that some - women and men - are "set apart" or called to ordained priesthood. There has also to be further reflection on Christian anthropology and what it means when we affirm that male and female are created in the image of God. Perhaps most importantly of all it requires an openness to the working of the Holy Spirit, in a reaffirmation of the doctrines, with the possibility of the development of the doctrines of the church in keeping with the times.

I believe it is appropriate to conclude with the words of Bishop Kallistos Ware, Bishop of Diokleia, who addresses the Orthodox churches, with words that are appropriate for all churches - those that ordain women and those, which do not. He writes: "In discussing the ministry of women in the Church, let us not be afraid (as Orthodox) to acknowledge that there is a mystery here which we have scarcely started to explore. In speaking of a 'mystery', I am using the word in its proper theological sense. A mystery is not just an enigma or an unsolved puzzle. It is a truth or a set of truths revealed by God to our created intelligence, yet never exhaus-